Living Beyond

"WHAT IF?"

Living Beyond

"WHAT IF?"

Release the Limits and Realize Your Dreams

DR. SHIRLEY DAVIS

Foreword by Les Brown

BK

Berrett–Koehler Publishers, Inc.

Berrett-Koehler Publishers, Inc.Tel: (510) 817-2277
1333 Broadway, Suite 1000   Fax: (510) 817-2278
Oakland, CA 94612-1921   www.bkconnection.com

ORDERING INFORMATION

Quantity sales. Special discounts are available on quantity purchases by corporations, associations, and others. For details, contact the "Special Sales Department" at the Berrett-Koehler address above.

Individual sales. Berrett-Koehler publications are available through most bookstores. They can also be ordered directly from Berrett-Koehler:
Tel: (800) 929-2929; Fax: (802) 864-7626; www.bkconnection.com.
Orders for college textbook/course adoption use. Please contact Berrett-Koehler:
Tel: (800) 929-2929; Fax: (802) 864-7626.

Distributed to the U.S. trade and internationally by Penguin Random House Publisher Services.

Berrett-Koehler and the BK logo are registered trademarks of Berrett-Koehler Publishers, Inc.

Printed in Canada.

Berrett-Koehler books are printed on long-lasting acid-free paper. When it is available, we choose paper that has been manufactured by environmentally responsible processes. These may include using trees grown in sustainable forests, incorporating recycled paper, minimizing chlorine in bleaching, or recycling the energy produced at the paper mill.

Library of Congress Cataloging-in-Publication Data

Names: Davis, Shirley, author. | Brown, Les, 1945-
    writer of foreword.
Title: Living beyond "what if?" : release the limits and realize your dreams /
    Dr. Shirley Davis ; foreword by Les Brown.
Description: First edition. | Oakland, CA : Berrett-Koehler Publishers, Inc., [2021] |
    Includes index.
Identifiers: LCCN 2021012883 | ISBN 9781523093267 (paperback) |
    ISBN 9781523093274 (adobe pdf) | ISBN 9781523093281 (epub)
Subjects: LCSH: Goal (Psychology) | Self-actualization (Psychology)
Classification: LCC BF505.G6 D38 2021 | DDC 158.1--dc23
LC record available at https://lccn.loc.gov/2021012883

First Edition

27 26 25 24 23 22 21   10 9 8 7 6 5 4 3 2 1

Book producer and text designer: Leigh McLellan Design.
Cover designer: Nita Ybarra. Cover photo: Nazrana Ferose.
Copyeditor: Alice Rowan. Proofreader: Mary Hazlewood. Indexer: Ken DellaPenta.

This book is dedicated to "the 90 percent"
—those who admit they are not living their best life because they are
chronic procrastinators and stuck at "What if?" and those who are living
with persistent fears that keep them parked on the side of the
road of life and not able to reach their destination.

To all who shared their stories, advice, endorsements,
and support, this book is dedicated to you.

CONTENTS

FOREWORD

by Les Brown

world renowned motivational speaker and best-selling author

*M*ost people live their lives daydreaming and saying, for example, "I wish I was rich," "I wish I could go back to school," "I wish I was married," or "I wish I had more free time." Einstein said "the imagination is a preview of the future."

Can you imagine yourself doing more and achieving greater things in life? Are you tired of putting your dreams on the shelf and hoping to get to them one day, only for days to turn into weeks, months, and then years? Maybe you're dreaming of starting your own business or trying to build up the courage to ask for a promotion or a pay increase. Maybe you are laid off and unemployment is about to run out, and so are your options. Maybe you've gotten stuck in a job where you work just hard enough not to get fired and they pay you just enough for you not to quit. If you are looking for some clues as to how to go from living a life of mediocrity to living a life beyond your limitations, you have just found the key in *Living Beyond "What If?"* by Dr. Shirley Davis.

My name is Les Brown. I am an international motivational speaker and trainer. I have been blessed to be able to change lives by telling my story and encouraging others to live their dreams. I have lived, learned, and earned, and now it is time to pass it on. Dr. Shirley Davis is an accomplished protégé, consummate professional, and now a good friend. She is a shining example of overcoming the odds and living her dreams.

Dr. Davis has put together a blueprint for success. She is very open and candid about the challenges and obstacles she has overcome to be the phenomenal businesswoman and global brand she is now. She is the right person to write this book.

Too many people barely scratch the surface of utilizing their imagination to change their destiny. It is also necessary to avoid procrastinating and to face your fears head on, because doing so builds character and inner strength. Dr. Davis examines the concepts of being stuck in life out of fear and making excuses for shortcomings. She provides some action steps for utilizing your imagination to create the life you've always dreamed of. She offers so many gems of wisdom that are invaluable for living your best life.

If you are seeking to change the direction of your life, this book is a must read! You have greatness within you! This is my story, this is Shirley's story, and we are sticking to it!

ARE YOU LIVING THE LIFE YOU'VE ALWAYS DREAMED OF?

e all dream, we all imagine, and we all plan. But why is it that some people achieve their dreams, and most do not?

For more than a decade I have been asking audiences all over the world two provocative questions:

1. Are you living the life you've always dreamed of?

2. If you got to live it over again, would you live it differently?

Surprisingly, only 10 percent of hands go up in response to the first question and 90 percent of hands go up for the second question. And when pressed on the second question, about what they would do differently, the most common responses are, "I would live my life with more passion, with purpose, with more intention, and without procrastination" and "I would live it with fewer regrets and I wouldn't waste time on the things that don't matter."

I know that feeling because for years I lived like the 90 percent. I didn't start out that way. As a kid I dreamed and imagined doing and being anything and going anywhere. There were no limitations, no fears, no worries, and nothing seemed impossible for me to achieve. I believed and lived like this throughout my childhood, until I reached early adulthood and went off to college. It was there that life started dealing me reality checks, upsets, and setbacks that disrupted my dreams and distorted my belief system.

That's what *Living Beyond "What If?"* is about. There are two parts to the book. Part 1 focuses on releasing the limits we place on ourselves as a result of life's crushing blows that test our faith, stamina, courage, strength, and resilience. How we respond to these challenges can determine the trajectory of our lives. We don't always know how our stories will end, but we can influence their direction by the choices we make, which are based on the beliefs we hold, and by the attitudes we adopt.

In an authentic way, I share how my own stories played out and shaped my life's trajectory. I suffered through and survived several near-death experiences, failed relationships, betrayal and broken trust, financial devastation, rejection, loneliness, career setbacks, and experiences of being minimized and marginalized, overlooked and undervalued, even while overperforming in many of my career roles. I was living neither my dreams nor the life I had imagined. In other words, I was living and surviving, but I wasn't thriving and enjoying life.

I detail how my dreams became overshadowed by hurt, disappointment, loss, grief, anger, self-doubt, brokenness, failure, insecurity, fear, and a lack of faith. These experiences caused me to place limits on myself and to ask the proverbial questions that begin with *What If?* What if I fail? What if I get rejected? What if I go broke? What if I get hurt? What if I succeed? I had so many disempowering conversations with myself that talked me out of seizing new opportunities, taking risks, and getting out of my own way. These conversations caused me to stay stuck at "one day I'm gonna," and as days turned into weeks and weeks turned into months and then months turned into years, I had yet to realize my dreams.

I wanted a better life, but for years I repeated a cycle and didn't know how to get out of it. If I didn't do something drastically different, I would be doomed to a life of regret. So I began my transformation. Part 1 details that journey and the steps I took to remove the self-imposed limitations of procrastination, fear, entertaining disempowering "What if?" beliefs, avoiding risk, and choosing bad company, and to rid myself of the toxic effects of these limitations.

Part 2 continues my journey beyond releasing the limitations and describes the long and difficult road I traveled to realize my dreams after many years of tears. Once I confronted the realities of my self-imposed obstacles, I started a new journey in search of significance. I reimagined my life by identifying my *why* and developed a life plan that would keep me focused and accountable. I grew up, and I became wiser. I started asking the right questions, I adopted the right mindset, I reevaluated my relationships, and I started making better choices. As life coach Iyanla Vanzant would say, "I did my work." Part 2 details for the reader the steps, strategies, and tactics I employed to get to where I am today.

The book cover says it all! The water is my happy place and where I found serenity in the midst of these life challenges. It was by the ocean that I dreamed, imagined, reflected, and reinvented myself. I hope that the woman you see on the cover exudes joy, peace, fulfillment, gratitude, and victory, because it is an image of my present reality and the woman I have become. I'm so thankful for the journey and the many lessons it taught me and the many gifts it deposited in me.

One of the biggest lessons and gifts I received from my experiences is that my life's journey is never *just about me.* It is about others. It is about you—special people who were assigned by destiny to cross my path in life and who needed to hear my story. I learned that my story is also your story, and your story is someone else's story. It is with that in mind that throughout this book I have included the stories of others who over the years were mentees, coaching clients, colleagues, and contacts. They granted me permission to share their stories because they agree that their stories are your stories.

They all faced battles similar to mine, and it is comforting to know I wasn't alone. They had a different set of circumstances but they have experienced similar effects and lessons that have shaped and guided their lives. They also embarked on their own journey toward releasing the limits in their lives so that they too could realize their dreams.

It is my belief that you didn't come across this book accidentally, because I believe everything happens for a reason. I believe our paths were meant to cross. It is my prayer that my story and the stories of others will bring you the inspiration, hope, and courage you need to start living beyond "What If?"

PART I

Release the Limits

Chapter 1

WAS IT JUST MY IMAGINATION?

What Is Imagination?

*I*magination is one of the most powerful tools that we have. It enables us to visualize the future. It is the doorway to unlimited possibilities and key to creating something more meaningful and significant. Simply defined, imagination is the ability of the mind to think in pictures, to conceive something that does not yet exist. It is a facet of the mind along with reason, emotions, and the will that allows us to contemplate our lives in the future.

We use our imagination all the time, whether we are daydreaming, planning, recalling, or meditating. Without imagination we would not have a source of creativity, because every innovation in history began with an image in someone's mind. Books, movies, toys, songs, automobiles, companies, foods, clothes, and phone apps and other technology advances, to name a few, all started in someone's imagination and without it we wouldn't enjoy the conveniences we do today.

Both individuals and organizations use their imagination to create their future state. For example, as a consultant I enjoy the opportunity to work with clients on developing their long-term strategic plans. I guide them through envisioning what the future could look like for them three to five years out. One of the first exercises I take them through involves using their imagination. I instruct them to "imagine that it is five years from now and your business has grown to a new level of success and profitability. Without being limited or constrained by budget, current practices, past successes, or the fear of failure, list all of the attributes of that new organization."

I have used the same exercise with individuals who are contemplating a strategic move and need to imagine their future. Taking them through this exercise sets a strong foundation on which they can build. Some of their best thinking is documented because they are given permission to imagine without limits or restrictions, just like we did as kids.

Dreaming as a Kid

Think back to when you were a kid and your dreams ran wild. What did you imagine being and doing, and where did you imagine going? I am a dreamer by nature and have a vivid imagination. As a child and up to my teenage years, I kept a diary and I remember writing all kinds of dreams about what I would be when I grew up. I wrote that I would be a teacher, an all-star athlete, a basketball coach, a high-fashion model in New York, a movie star, a lawyer, and a writer. I imagined being rich and living like what I had seen on the TV show starring Robin Leach, *Lifestyles of the Rich and Famous*. My imagination transported me to places all over the world, to achieving anything my heart desired and my mind envisioned. I was unrestricted by rules and had no limits, questions, or fears. Nothing seemed impossible.

Most of these dreams were influenced by what I watched on TV, by what I was taught by my parents, and by what came naturally to me—for example, teaching. I loved playing "school" with my three brothers and being the teacher. We would play for hours and I would actually create assignments for them to do and games for them to play. I would assign them homework and grade their papers, so dreaming of being a teacher one day wasn't farfetched. It would end up being my job as a trainer years later.

I loved to play "dress up" with my mom's clothes and shoes, put on her makeup and jewelry, and pretend to be a model and a contestant in beauty pageants. During those years, I watched TV shows like *Star Search* every week and the Miss America and Miss USA pageants every year and imagine myself being one of the contestants. Modeling on stage also came naturally to me. I started modeling for a local agency and participated in a number of fashion shows, and even won a local *Star Search* runway modeling competition. I didn't become a high-fashion model in New York for a world-renowned designer, but my dream of modeling was partially realized.

While watching the pageants every year I was enamored with the parade of costumes, the extravagant gowns, the roaring applause from each contestant's cheering section, the speech competitions, and the amazing talent performances. And then the big moment came when the winner's name was announced and this huge crown, decorated with what looked like hundreds of diamonds and rubies, was placed on the winner's head. I was hooked. As I watched those pageants, I would think, "I can do that. They walk across the stage, they have a speech competition, and they perform a talent. Yes, I can do that." I started dreaming and imagining that one day I could be Miss _____.

At the age of 14, I competed in my first local pageant, because it had a speech competition and because I had grown fond of the stage. I was already playing sports and was quite competitive, and now I had started modeling, so I thought I had a good shot. Even though I had never competed in a pageant before, I had watched enough of them on TV and had convinced myself that if I were good at modeling I could be good at pageants too. Besides, this pageant offered scholarship money for college and a variety of great gifts, and if I won I would have the opportunity to sport a huge rhinestone crown like I had seen on TV.

Turns out that my dreams were not too lofty, because in my first pageant I placed second runner-up, won the speech competition, and received positive feedback from the judges regarding my interview and stage presence. The pageant director and the judges strongly urged me to come back to compete again the following year and told me I had a good chance of winning. So I did. I spent the entire next year reading, staying abreast of current events, soul searching to get clarity on my platform, and practicing my interview skills. I also kept good grades, which was a requirement because it was a scholarship pageant. The preparation paid off because the next year I competed again and won my first title, Miss District of Columbia National Teenager.

My parents enrolled me and my brothers in sports at early ages. I played softball and basketball and ran track. These also came naturally to me and I got really good. Playing with my brothers taught me to be tough and to play more competitively. By the time I reached high school I had already played for the local Boys and Girls Club and had achieved all-star status in softball, track, and basketball. I didn't reach my goal of being a coach but I was captain of my softball team, so I guess that was close enough. I tried out for the varsity teams in high school and was selected. As I achieved some of those childhood dreams, I built up a lot of confidence and assurance, which reinforced that nothing was impossible when I put my mind to something. So I continued to imagine and add more dreams to my list.

In high school I started dating and eventually experienced my first love. Then I began imagining getting married to the man of my dreams, having a family, and living happily ever after like I had seen in many love stories on TV, in the movies, and in teenage novels. When I went off to college, I majored in pre-law and imagined myself being a top prosecutor and then a family court judge. I was still dating my high school sweetheart and we were going strong. He was attending another college five hours from me on a basketball scholarship and was in his second year. He would drive to my college to see me and I would drive to as many of his games as I could to support him. We were talking about getting married after graduation and it appeared that more of my dreams would be realized.

When Life Happens and Dreams Are Shattered

Life Event I: My First Heartbreak

Then a series of unexpected turns, tragedies, and transitions shook me to my core and redefined the trajectory of my life. The first event happened at the end of my first year of college, when my boyfriend became aloof and started acting a bit strange. He wasn't calling as much and started making excuses as to why he couldn't come to visit. When I would ask him what was going on, he would just shrug it off. The clincher came when we had planned to hang out for the summer break and he decided it wasn't a good idea anymore. Finally I confronted him and demanded an explanation, and he admitted he had "found somebody else."

I was devastated. We had made so many plans and he had seemed so committed to our dreams. I had been sure that he loved me, which he told me often, but now he was telling me he was with someone else. I was angry, confused, broken, and shocked all at the same time. This was the first time I had really fallen in love and the first time I had experienced this kind of hurt. My heart was shattered into a hundred pieces and everything we had dreamed together was now turning into a nightmare.

It took a while to get over the hurt, but after getting more engrossed in college life (attending campus fraternity and sorority parties, focusing on my major, holding down a part-time job, and hanging out with new friends), I moved on. In my last year of college I met a guy through mutual friends. We hit it off quickly and began dating. Eventually we fell head over heels for each other and I began imagining my life with him.

We dreamed of moving to Tulsa, Oklahoma where I would do graduate work in religious studies and he would complete his undergraduate degree. We both dreamed of having children and living happily ever after. We had no money, but we had a whole lot of hope that everything would be alright simply because we were people of faith and we were in love. After I graduated from my undergraduate degree program at the University of Maryland, we worked to make our plans and dreams a reality, and things seemed to be falling into place, or so I thought.

Life Event 2: Near-Death Car Crash

The second event happened in the summer I graduated from college. I was still planning to move to Oklahoma and start my graduate program, but I had never been there. Three girlfriends and I decided to take our first cross-country trip, from Maryland to Oklahoma. This trip was a great opportunity to check things out. We made the twenty-one-hour drive and arrived safely. During the five-day visit we had a blast. My closest girlfriend decided to check out the school for her own graduate studies as well, so we attended orientation sessions together, toured the campus, met our professors, made new friends, found an apartment near campus, signed the lease, and registered for the fall semester. We didn't want to leave but were so excited to return as roommates and grad students and start the next chapter in our lives. While we attended orientations, our two other girlfriends explored the city, did some shopping, and attended the conference with us every evening.

It came time to return to Maryland. We reluctantly loaded up the car and began the drive back to the East Coast. Not being much of a long-distance driver, I sat in the back seat on the passenger side. With three other people who could drive for hours at a time, I knew we would be on the East Coast before it was my turn to get behind the wheel. I don't remember what happened from this point on, but I am sharing this story as it was told to me.

My friend and I had been asleep for hours in the backseat when at approximately two o'clock in the morning our lives changed forever. We had started in Tulsa and reached West Virginia. The highway we were on was a narrow two-lane road with very few cars traveling in the wee hours of the morning. It was under construction. The shoulder of the road was blocked off by a concrete barricade lined with orange and white striped cans. It was pitch black with no street lighting.

Sometime around two o'clock the driver pulled off onto the side of the road to switch with the other front-seat passenger. I remained in the back seat, asleep. My girlfriend sitting beside me woke up during the driver switch. As the car got back onto the road and headed east, the one who had now taken the wheel realized she had not buckled her seat belt, so she reached down to lock it. Seconds later she looked up and saw the car heading into the concrete barricade and the orange and white cans. She violently turned the steering wheel to the extreme right to avoid the concrete barricades, and lost control of the car.

The car flipped over and careened down an embankment to several feet below the highway. The driver, who had just buckled her seat belt, was shaken and received some scrapes and bruises. The front-seat passenger hit her head on the windshield, shattering the glass. The car flipped a second and third time, ejecting me headfirst through the back window. The car flipped a fourth time and landed on its side twenty feet down the embankment. It was now a mangled mess of steel and broken glass. The driver was still seated under the wheel. The police speculated that the buckled seat belt saved her life.

Bloody and bruised, the driver began to scream for each of us to identify our location. Darkness made it impossible to see each other. Our voices were the only way to signal where we were. They called out for each other until they were able to hold hands. One, two, three accounted for. But where was Shirley? "Shirley, where are you? Please answer." Their cries went unheard.

One of the passengers later recounted that she got down on her hands and knees and crawled around on the ground trying to feel for me. Hurt and bleeding, wading through broken glass in the darkness, her efforts were futile. The driver ran in the direction of the highway. One car had already passed us by with no knowledge we were stranded down the embankment, twenty feet away. Our driver stood by the side of the highway and frantically waited for the next car or truck.

Within minutes, an eighteen-wheeled tractor trailer sped her way. The trucker, with his lights on high beam, spotted her waving her arms in the air and jumping up and down in a panic. He stopped. He immediately radioed in a call to the local police, then grabbed his flashlight from the truck and helped the women search the area for me. I was found thirty feet from the automobile, motionless and unresponsive, covered in glass and weeds, bleeding from my head and arms. The flashlight beamed into my face. I did not move. My friends continued to call my name. I was still breathing, but no one knew the extent of my injuries, so they did not move me.

Moments later sirens sounded in the distance. Two of the passengers and the trucker ran to flag down the police and ambulances. The flashlight and the truck's high beams were the source of light for the emergency brigade. Within minutes two additional ambulances arrived to transport the four of us to the medical center in Wheeling, West Virginia. We arrived at the hospital emergency room in less than 30 minutes.

According to my friends the hospital was very quiet that night and visiting hours had long since ended. The atmosphere abruptly changed when we were brought into the emergency room. Nurses and doctors were standing by and had been thoroughly briefed on our condition by the EMTs. Our vital signs were checked by the hospital staff. We were wheeled into separate exam rooms and immediately examined for internal bleeding, broken bones, and concussions. I was still unconscious. I have no recollection of my time in the emergency room.

The next morning the police investigated the scene of the accident and, after viewing the massive amounts of glass and shredded steel, shook their heads in disbelief that anyone could have survived. That same morning the headline news reported, "Four Women Survive an Early Morning Car Accident". The report stated, "It was a miracle that anyone survived since the car was so demolished," and "God was apparently in the car with the young women." The story went on to report that "police officers found nearly half a dozen Bibles scattered about the scene that apparently had fallen out of the car during the crash." What a testimony! A news report of a car crash that spoke of a miracle by God! The other ladies watched the amazing story from their hospital beds. I was still unconscious.

By the next morning, friends and relatives of the driver had driven from Washington, D.C., to the hospital. The driver and the other conscious passengers shared the details of the accident. Several women surrounded my bed and began to pray. They continued praying without ceasing. I started to hear noises but couldn't make out anything, nor could I open my eyes. I remember that one of the women pulled my arm as if to lift me up. I slowly awoke from my comatose state.

A few minutes later I opened my eyes and saw strange people standing around me in a chain of locked hands. I had no idea where I was or what had happened. I remember looking at the clock in the room and seeing that it was 3:00, but I didn't know what day it was or how long I had been there. The last thing I remembered prior to this was being asleep in the back seat of the car. When I awoke, I began to ask for details about what had happened and where we were. The nurses later explained that I had suffered a severe head concussion, received ten stitches in my forehead and twenty in my right side, and had glass lodged in various parts of my body, including my scalp.

We went home to Maryland two days later under my doctor's and parents' care. Over the next few weeks I would feel a sharp pain while washing up (I couldn't take a shower for several weeks due to my injuries); it was glass working its way out of my body. The glorious news is that I had no internal bleeding and no major organs were damaged. I was badly bruised and severely stiff, had scars in many places, and was in a lot of pain, but I was determined to get better so that I could move to Oklahoma.

I had not forgotten the amazing experience we had while attending the college weekend orientation. I remembered the peace and excitement that had come over me while I was there. But as I recovered on the couch at my parents' home, I spent hours wondering, what if my dreams were just a figment of my imagination? Would they actually come true? I wondered, What if I had lost a limb, lost my sight or my hearing, or worse, lost my life? Since I had come so close, I began to think about how precious life was and that I couldn't take anything for granted. I was sure I wanted to move to Oklahoma and start graduate school. A month later the doctor released me to travel and complete my recovery and therapy there. So my mom, my brother, and I loaded up my car and made the twenty-one-hour cross-country trip from Maryland to Oklahoma. I was excited to start this new chapter in my life.

Life Event 3: Getting Married, Getting Divorced, and Having a Baby, in That Order

My first year in graduate school was amazing. I made lots of new friends; I adored my professors; my boyfriend, who had now become my fiancé, had moved to Oklahoma as well; and I had been hired at a local bank. That following summer, my fiancé and I got married. We didn't have a lot of money, but we had faith, love, and each other, and we thought we could conquer the world. As I write about this more than thirty years later, it sounds so cheesy and childish, but it seemed real at the time. What was also real was that we didn't want to take life for granted, especially since I had experienced the near-death car accident the year before.

When we told our parents about our marriage plans, they warned against it insisting that we were too young. My fiancé's parents went even further, insisting he was not ready to take care of another person and needed time to mature. We ignored their warnings and chalked it up to them being overprotective because they had gotten married at the same age we were. I planned the wedding all summer, and that August, before we went back to college, we got married at our local church in Maryland, and then returned to Oklahoma.

Five years later we would prove our parents right. Our lack of maturity, ongoing problems and disagreements about money (or the lack thereof), unrealistic expectations, and unwillingness to accept responsibility drove a wedge between us. Love and faith were not enough. I resented bearing the brunt of the responsibility and not feeling valued. On top of that we had not developed proper conflict management skills and thus were constantly bickering and blaming each other.

As we made the decision to terminate the marriage I found out I was pregnant, again. Two years earlier I had suffered a miscarriage and was devastated as I went through that loss. This time I was thrilled to be past my first trimester and all was well, but at the same time I was having a baby while facing the prospect of raising it as a single parent.

We went back and forth and considered working things out but our talks fell apart again and again. He moved on to dating someone one else and I decided that trying to fix the marriage just because I was pregnant was not going to fix all of the issues between us. It would only exacerbate the situation and put a child in the middle. So I went through with the divorce, after much consternation.

Talk about shattered dreams and all the things I had imagined my life to be! We had dreamed about living happily ever after—not going through a miscarriage, experiencing financial bankruptcy, or having a child while going through a divorce and raising that child apart from each other. If anyone had told me this would be my reality, I would have cursed the ground they were standing on. But this is where I found my life. It was another defining moment that caused me to ask again if my dreams were just figments of my imagination.

Going through the divorce affected my self-confidence, sense of self-worth, and ability to trust and to believe in my dreams, for years. But I didn't have time to stop and grieve, be bitter, or try to deal out revenge. I was about to have a baby. I was faced with all the challenges of single parenting, but mostly I was faced with extensive financial obligations.

I would characterize myself as being flat broke, living paycheck to paycheck, not being able to make ends meet, and operating with a poverty mindset.

I had a lot of debt (grad school loans, credit cards, a car payment, rent, and other loans), and I was behind on most of them. I was borrowing money and getting cash advances from high-interest credit cards, taking out loans from check-cashing companies, and borrowing money from agencies that would take your car title as collateral. I was selling personal property (jewelry, a stereo system, designer purses) at pawnshops just to pay basic bills, and I was getting high-interest-rate loans—at 25 to 30 percent—while not knowing how I was going to repay them.

My daughter was born six months after I filed for divorce, and while she was the best gift I'd ever been given, I also felt the weight of the world on my shoulders trying to take care of her. I was in bondage (mentally, emotionally, and financially), I was stressed out, I was losing weight, I felt hopeless, and I was alone. One day I got tired of being sick and tired. I had been living this way for years and I really didn't know how I was going to make ends meet. So I did what many of us have done in this situation.

I prayed that famous prayer, "God, if you get me out of this, I promise I'll never get into it again." I had prayed it before, but this time, I meant it. I had hit rock bottom and I needed a miracle. I promised God and my daughter that I was going to get out of debt. I was going to do whatever it took to make the shifts and changes I needed to make to get out of this cycle and pit of despair and desperation.

My ex-husband (my daughter's dad) had moved on and remarried, and we were not on good terms. But regardless, I had someone depending on me and, if I wanted better for my life, I would have to make changes. I would have to make some sacrifices, and some difficult choices. That meant getting some counseling and coaching, having some accountability. It meant taking control of the way I was living and of my financial situation. It meant I had to go through a process, with a step-by-step plan. It meant having the right resources and the right people around me. And most important, it meant adopting a new and different mindset. I wished that all of my situation was just a bad dream, but it wasn't. It was real and present.

Life Event 4: Bank Robbery

The fourth experience came when I was working at a bank as a supervisor while living in Tulsa, Oklahoma. It was 9:00 a.m. and I had just opened the front doors for the few customers waiting outside. I stopped at the supply closet near the doors to get a few pens and some packs of tape for the teller machines. At 9:03 a.m. three masked gunmen stormed through the doors. Two of them rushed to the teller line and jumped over the counter. The third one grabbed me, pointed his gun directly at my forehead, and yelled at everyone in the bank, "If anyone in here moves I will blow her brains out." He was talking about me. All I could see were two barrels pointed right between my eyes, and even though the gun wasn't touching my skin, my two eyes made direct contact with the two silver barrels.

Immediately I was gripped with fear and couldn't move, think, or comprehend what to do. My body fell onto the floor and into a fetal position on my side. All I could do was pray. Once I hit the floor I couldn't see where the gun was pointed, but seconds later the gunman yelled again, "I told you, if anyone in here moves I will blow her brains out." I could hear his voice above me, so I knew the gun must have still been pointed at my head.

An indescribable fear hit me again and I began to brace myself to be killed. I prayed harder, as if with my last breath. Within a few seconds I heard footsteps running from behind the teller line, and then I heard his footsteps move away from me and toward the door.

The next sound I heard was the front door shutting. I didn't move immediately. I was still paralyzed with fear and not 100 percent sure the bank robbers had really run out. Others in the bank began to move and speak, and someone yelled, "Lock the door." I turned over slowly from my fetal position and waited for the customer who had yelled to lock the door. As I heard the deadbolt click, I started to get up, but I couldn't stand up straight. I was in disbelief, shock, and fear like I had never before experienced. For a moment it felt like I was living a bad dream—a nightmare—and I tried to wake up from it but I couldn't. Even now, as I tell this story, I can still see the event vividly in my mind.

So many questions flooded my mind after that experience. The next day when I woke up I wondered, Did I just have a nightmare? Did I really live through a bank robbery? Had I again survived a life-and-death situation like the car crash? What was God trying to tell me? What could I have done differently that morning? What if I had been shot? Would I have died with regrets and a lot of dreams unfulfilled? What if they never catch the bank robbers? How will I go back to work each day without fearing they would rob us again? What if I should be doing something else with my life?

More Hard Lessons Learned Sooner

Over the next seven years, I experienced more turns, twists, and transitions in my life that continued to cause me to wonder if my dreams would ever come true or were just figments of my imagination. A few years after the divorce I accepted a new job that relocated me back to the East Coast. It felt like a fresh start for me and my daughter. Life eventually stabilized. I had been through financial counseling and had worked out a plan to get out of debt and improve my credit rating. Some of my financial obligations had been written off. Others were on a payment plan. I was now making enough money to pay my bills, but more important, I was keeping my promise to God and to my daughter not to get into that kind of debt again.

I opened up my heart to trust again and got back on the dating scene. It was a bit challenging having a young child and trying to juggle new relationships, so I was more guarded, or so I thought. I ended up learning more heart lessons, but interestingly enough I was learning hard lessons sooner. One guy I got involved with turned out to be a master manipulator. He was able to identify my weaknesses and vulnerabilities by listening adeptly and keenly to where I had the greatest needs, and he was skillful in tapping into those things. He wined and dined me and gave me wonderful gifts. He said and did all the right things.

But I found out that he had no intention of being in a committed, monogamous relationship. When you learn that the person giving you all these gifts and planning this great life with you is also telling five or six other women the same thing, it can make you feel completely insignificant. It was hurtful, but it wasn't the end of the world, and I quickly moved on because I had a daughter to raise and I didn't want her to be exposed to that drama. There would be a repeat performance with several other suitors, but each time I was keen to move on when they showed their true colors, and I took an assessment of the lessons I had learned.

The first lesson was that I recognized a flaw in me. I've always prided myself on being the kind of person who looks for the best in other people and assumes positive intent. This has worked in my favor in some instances and against me in others. In this case, I realized that I attracted and settled for men who were either very needy or insecure and used me as a crutch and a caregiver.

I didn't know at first that the person wasn't healthy for me, because I took their words as truth and didn't see the facade until I was well into the relationship and had become emotionally invested. By then it was too late to back out easily. I tried to make it work by trying to change them for the better. This wasn't an implausible approach because by nature I am a caring, generous, nurturing soul and have the heart of a teacher, a coach, and a missionary. So while I learned more about why I chose the kind of men I did, I still had work to do to avoid being a magnet for that kind of man.

A second lesson was that I learned to open my eyes wider and not get so involved too quickly; I learned to step back and observe behavior more and ask more questions. I started introducing my serious dates to my closest friends sooner so they could observe and give me objective feedback. Most important, I learned never to underestimate the power of my inner voice. On several occasions it sent me a message that something wasn't right about a person, but I ignored the warnings and drowned out the voice with my own rationalizations.

There were more lessons. I learned never to be so needy or so lonely that I would settle for crumbs and compromise my value. I recognized that I must not allow the external things I am looking for to overshadow the things that count the most—things that are matters of the heart and soul —such as integrity, honesty, character, trust, respect, commitment, and the like.

I learned these hard heart lessons after living through abusive, disruptive, and hurtful situations that could have left me bitter, unstable, addicted, in prison, in a mental institution, or dead. Nevertheless, I survived.

Wanting Better in Life

These experiences that happened right out of college and into my early adulthood were defining moments in my life. They shook my foundation and introduced me to the real world. They hijacked the dreams and imaginations I'd had as a kid and overshadowed my innocent belief that anything was possible. As I moved into my thirties I was battling the effects of my twenties. Those years had eroded my trust, diminished my self-assurance, caused me to build walls of protection around me, and led me to adopt many disempowering beliefs and insecurities about myself. But I didn't want to become one of those people who died at age 30 and waited to get buried at age 85—just existing but not living.

I wasn't pleased with my life or where I was headed, but I was grateful to be alive. I could have been killed on several occasions, but my life was spared. I didn't want to take life for granted, and I knew that if God had allowed me to live and to survive the many tragedies I had already suffered, then He had a plan for my life. I just had to figure out what that was.

I had to take a journey of self-development in order to get to self-actualization. I knew it wouldn't be easy, quick, or pain free. It was going to take time, honesty, and courage. I had a lot to unpack and a lot to bury. I wanted to dream again and not allow my past to make my dreams mere figments of my imagination. I wanted to believe they could become reality. I wanted to heal from the pain of my past and the effects of my poor choices. I needed to explore, expose, and then expel the self-imposed limits I had placed on myself. And I had to get out of my own way so I could start living the life I was destined to live.

Here begins my journey.

Chapter 2

THE #1 REASON
WE DON'T REALIZE OUR DREAMS

*W*hy are most people not living their dreams or their best life? If you guessed, *procrastination*, you are correct. Procrastination continues to be the number one reason that dreams go unrealized. In this chapter I explain some of the science and psychology of the reasons we procrastinate. I then identify the most common tasks on which we procrastinate and some strategies for releasing the limitations of procrastination.

What Is Procrastination?

This topic is certainly not new. It has been studied for centuries, especially related to *why* people procrastinate. Simply put, procrastination is avoiding doing something that should get done. It is putting off a decision or an action for one reason or another. Writer Eric Jaffe defines procrastination as "the voluntary delay of some important task that we intend to do, despite knowing that we'll suffer as a result." He goes on to quote researcher Joseph Ferrari, a fellow of the Association for Psychological Science and professor of psychology at DePaul University, who says that "while everybody may procrastinate, not everyone is a procrastinator."[1]

If you're honest with yourself, you can acknowledge that at some point in your life you put off doing something that you knew needed to be done.

It can be as simple as taking out the trash, cleaning your room, washing the car, or studying for an exam. It could be bigger tasks such as going to the doctor for a yearly exam, responding to a legal action, or filing your taxes. And if we are putting off these simple and bigger tasks, it's likely we are also putting off the even bigger tasks that are tied directly to realizing our dreams, which can include going back to school, asking for that promotion, applying for that new job, or starting a family.

Here I share Meghana Joshi's story because she admits that procrastinating on the simple and bigger tasks blocked opportunities for her to become a licensed architect, which kept her stuck and frustrated for more than a decade. She shares how she finally cracked the code on her procrastination, which ultimately cracked the glass ceiling on her career.

Meghana's Story

"HOW BAD DO I WANT IT?"

Meghana was born and raised in India and immigrated to the United States after graduating from college with her bachelor's degree in architecture. She tried finding a job in this field and found out she had to go through licensure. She also had to complete additional education requirements because the architecture program she attended in India taught about concrete and steel structures, but the program in which she studied in California taught mostly about wood structures. So she had to relearn a few things in order to qualify for her licensing exam.

She had a child and became the primary caretaker and found herself having to juggle the responsibilities of working, parenting, and studying for her exam. It was a difficult transition that would cause her to put her dream of getting licensed on hold. She asked herself many "What if?" questions such as, What if I fail the exams? What if I never get licensed? and What if I don't have time? Year after year, on January 1st she would commit that this would be the year she would finish her exam and get licensed. She would study for the first few days but then get sidetracked.

Finally, after nearly a decade of continuously hitting a glass ceiling in her career, she got serious about getting her license. Not having a license blocked her from moving into middle management positions. This realization forced her to commit fully to getting it done. By then her daughter was in high school and she was determined to get her license before her daughter graduated. She'd had five years to finish seven tests and she was approaching her fourth year. She was scheduled to take her last exam when the school decided to go from one version to another version of the test.

At the same time, her mom suffered a heart attack in India and Meghana traveled back home to be with her. When she returned to San Francisco she had to be transitioned to the new version of the test, which required two more steps in licensing. Needless to say, Meghana was quite frustrated. She had two years to finish, and with the new requirements she started procrastinating again. The exam remained on her to-do list, but work had now turned into ten-hour days, her daughter was more involved in activities at school, and Meghana was focused on everything else but studying.

She hit her glass ceiling a second time, knowing she could not move up in her career without that credential next to her name. She was desperate, feeling hopeless and frustrated, all at the same time. Seeing how full her days were between six o'clock in the morning and nine o'clock at night, it looked impossible for her to study for her exams. She finally came to a breaking point and asked herself, "How bad do you want this?"

In her desperation she got creative. She realized she needed to use her early morning hours to study. Trying to find two hours in the evening didn't work because then she was focused on fixing dinner and helping her daughter with homework, and she was tired from a long workday. So she committed to waking up at 4:00 in the morning and studying until 6:00 a.m. She found that these two hours were uninterrupted; the house was quiet, she didn't turn on her phone, and she was focused and rested. Her commitment paid off this time.

Over the next six weeks, Meghana completed her last two exams, submitted all of the required documentation, and finally earned her architect's license. Additionally, she has continued her routine of waking up at 4:00 o'clock in the morning and uses that time to focus on herself and complete other tasks. She is excited about her next step, which is to seek a promotion. She has secured mentors in the architecture field to guide her through this process, because the field is male dominated. She has also made another bold move and drafted an email to her supervisor indicating her interest in moving into a management role in the future. She has put herself out there and that is to be applauded after all she has been through.

When I asked Meghana what she learned about herself through this process, she responded that she used to write out her goals and if they were too big she would procrastinate because she didn't feel she had time to complete them. Now she approaches goals in smaller steps and every day does something toward reaching them, no matter how small.

She also learned she had to want something bad enough in order to make the sacrifices and time to get it done. She did something different in order to get a different outcome. She changed her daily routine, which has now become a ritual for her being more productive and completing more of her goals. Meghana is optimistic about her future and proud of her accomplishment of becoming a licensed architect.

What Do You Procrastinate on the Most?

When I decided to write this book, I took a personal inventory of the things I've been most guilty of procrastinating on over the years. I also surveyed hundreds of people in my network and in my audiences and conducted Google searches to identify the tasks that people most commonly procrastinate on. Following is a summary of those tasks (not ranked in any order). In the spirit of transparency, I have placed an asterisk beside the items that are mine. You too may place an asterisk beside the tasks that you know you have been guilty of procrastinating on the most over the years. If some are missing, feel free to write them down.

- Going to the gym/physical exercise*
- Doing homework or studying for an exam*
- Paying bills*

- Answering emails
- Returning phone calls*
- Making/keeping doctor appointments
- Completing home projects*
- Cleaning
- Eating healthier/avoiding junk food
- Returning to college to finish a degree
- Getting car repairs done*
- Apologizing to someone
- Quitting smoking or drinking
- Spending time with the kids
- Learning a second language*
- Giving feedback/criticism
- Starting a business*
- Cleaning out the clutter (on your desk or in your home)*
- Running a marathon
- Writing a book*
- Ending a bad relationship*
- Going to church

My many asterisks admit that I have put off so many things over the years that I wish I hadn't—the simple, the big, and those tasks tied to my dreams. I put off writing books, launching my business, doing projects around the house, checking in with certain friends and family members, paying off credit cards, getting dental work done, taking care of repairs on my car, leaving jobs, ending bad relationships, having difficult conversations—and the list goes on. Procrastinating on some of these tasks had very serious consequences that affected my relationships, my credit standing, my health, my peace of mind, my performance, and my sense of accomplishment.

What were the consequences of the tasks you have been guilty of procrastinating on most over the years? Which are simple, big, or tied directly to realizing your dreams? More important, ask yourself, *Why* do you keep procrastinating, and *how* could you stop?

Why We Procrastinate—Present Self vs. Future Self

James Clear, the *New York Times* best-selling author of *Atomic Habits*, shares one of the most practical insights in terms of our brain function that explains why we procrastinate. He compares the dichotomy of our Present Self versus our Future Self:

> Research has revealed a phenomenon called "time inconsistency," which helps explain why procrastination seems to pull us in, despite our good intentions. Time inconsistency refers to the tendency of the human brain to value immediate rewards more highly than future rewards.
>
> The best way to understand this is by imagining that you have two selves: your Present Self and your Future Self. When you set goals for yourself—like losing weight or writing a book or learning a language—you are actually making plans for your Future Self. You are envisioning what you want your life to be like in the future. Researchers have found that when you think about your Future Self, it is quite easy for your brain to see the value in taking actions with long-term benefits. The Future Self values long-term rewards.
>
> However, while the Future Self can set goals, only the Present Self can take action. When the time comes to make a decision, you are no longer making a choice for your Future Self. Now you are in the present moment, and your brain is thinking about the Present Self. Researchers have discovered that the Present Self really likes instant gratification, not long-term payoff. So, the Present Self and the Future Self are often at odds with one another. The Future Self wants to be trim and fit, but the Present Self wants a donut. Sure, everyone knows you should eat healthy today to avoid being overweight in 10 years. But consequences like an increased risk for diabetes or heart failure are years away.[2]

After reading his work, it makes more sense that for years I put my dreams on pause and that many people don't realize their dreams. In my brain, my future state was at odds with my present state. I could see my future but I was living in my present. When we procrastinate, we pass the buck to our Future Self. I really did want to accomplish those dreams. I really did see myself in that future state. But I was in a battle between setting goals (my Future Self) and taking action (my Present Self), and often my Present Self won.

In my work as a consultant I am frequently called on to assist organizations in establishing more inclusive, respectful, and high-performing workplace cultures. An important aspect of that work is helping leaders understand what unconscious bias is and how a part of our brain functions in a way that causes us to react quickly, without rationale, and to make snap judgments that can be riddled with bias. That part of our brain is called the amygdala. It is the deepest part of the limbic system, which regulates our emotions.

However, another part of our brain is designed to help us slow down, be more mindful, and make more rational decisions. It is called the prefrontal neocortex. I studied brain science for more than ten years to prepare for the work I do. I referred back to it when I began my research for this book, and I discovered more fascinating information that I didn't see before about how the way our brain functions may explain why we procrastinate. Here's what I found in an article called "Want to Train Your Brain to Stop Procrastinating? Read These Tips from a Neuroscientist":

> Science explains procrastination as the fight sparked between two parts of the brain when it's faced with an unpleasant activity or assignment: It's a battle of the limbic system (the unconscious zone that includes the pleasure center) and the prefrontal cortex (a much more recently evolved part of the brain that's basically your internal "planner"). When the limbic system wins, which is often, the result is putting off for tomorrow what could (and should) be done today—which offers temporary relief from that unpleasant feeling of needing and, for whatever reason, not wanting to do something. The prefrontal cortex is a newer and weaker portion

of the brain that allows you to integrate information and make decisions. It gets the job done. But there's nothing automatic about its function: You have to kick it into gear. The moment you're not consciously engaged in a task, your limbic system takes over, and you give in to what feels good, which is anything but that book report—you procrastinate.[3]

Procrastination will never allow you to live the life you've always dreamed of living. It is an epidemic that can be cured and corrected only if the root causes are discovered and conquered. For years my dreams went unfulfilled because I didn't seek to understand the underlying reasons I procrastinated. In fact, I didn't consider it procrastination as much as considered my dreams to be too lofty, and I allowed my circumstances at the time to dictate my future.

I also justified my lack of follow-through by admitting I had too much on my plate already, I would never be able to finance those dreams, and they would take too much time, effort, and energy and might not work out anyway. How many of us do this? These are the limitations we place on ourselves, and it is these that we need to release if we ever want our dreams to see the light of day. Procrastination is a result of the many disempowering questions we ask ourselves and of the types of rationalization we use as excuses to put our dreams on hold. (We'll explore these disempowering questions in the next chapter).

The Psychology of Present Bias

In addition to the science of procrastination, there's another, similar concept that further underscores why we procrastinate. It's called the psychology of present bias. Ever heard of it? It is when we settle for a smaller present reward rather than wait for a larger future reward. When considering trade-offs between two future moments, people tend to give stronger weight to the payoff that is closer to the present.[4] Therefore, people are biased toward the present.

Think about people who win the Powerball or Mega Millions jackpot. They are given two options for collecting their winnings—the lump sum or the annuity payment. A lump-sum payout distributes the full amount of after-tax winnings at once. The annuity option provides annual payments over time (usually thirty years). Can you guess which option most winners take? The one that pays out all of the money at once, even though it's a lesser amount than they would receive if they took the annuity payout. This is a prime example of present bias. Many studies have been conducted that given participants the choice to take the immediate reward or wait for a larger reward in the future. Again, the choice made is usually the immediate reward.

My Present Bias Delayed My Dream of Starting a Business

As I shared earlier, one of the dreams I wrote down year after year was launching my own business. I knew I wanted to be my own boss and do training, consulting, and coaching. I was already doing it in my full-time roles as a human resources (HR) professional, director of training and development, and global head of diversity and inclusion. I loved the work I did and enjoyed the people I worked with and those I served. But I still felt like something was missing. I felt limited and confined to a job description in each role. I wanted to do bigger and broader things, and in reality I was making someone else's dream come true, not mine.

I was working long hours, making a lot of sacrifices, traveling across the country, yet not feeling valued or appreciated for my contributions. I was still dealing with the organizational politics and the constant bureaucracy that stood in the way of getting things done. On top of that, I still had to fight against biases, stereotypes, and prejudgments not only because of my particular diversities (a woman, a person of color, a single mom, a woman of faith, and so on), but also because of the nature of the work I did (HR and diversity, and equity and inclusion work, which has been perceived as controversial, scary, and uncomfortable, so it has not always been met with open arms).

Each year when I wrote down this dream of launching my own business, it was real for me. I was excited when I went through my mental checklist of all the great things I could have by launching my business.

I could run it without the limitations of having a boss (and even worse, having a bad boss), dealing with company politics, or being overlooked for a well-deserved promotion or pay increase. I could have complete autonomy and creative authority to develop my own products and services, and they would be mine. I could create something that utilized all of my skills, talents, experiences, and passions. I could wake up every day and feel a sense of pride in seeing my company make a transformational impact. I could have something to pass on as a legacy. I saw limitless possibilities in launching my own business—but it was in the future.

I would then think about the six-figure income I was currently making, the steady paycheck I received every two weeks, the great health benefits the company offered, the five weeks of paid vacation, the tuition reimbursement I enjoyed, and many other perks that came with being a senior executive, and my dream would suddenly seem too daunting and risky. Besides, I had a daughter who would be going off to college in a few years and I needed to save. I had a home loan, a car payment, and other bills, and I enjoyed a comfortable lifestyle. This is what present bias looks like. When I considered my future and compared the past and the present, I put stronger weight on the payoffs that were closer to the present and not so far off, and ultimately talked myself out of that dream for years.

Don't get me wrong. I am a big believer in timing is everything, and so is planning. I believe there are a season and a time for every purpose. I believe that everything happens for a reason and that, in the end, the lessons and growth that come from all of our experiences can work in our favor, but we have to make the decision and be committed to the process of self-development. And we must do the work.

I realize now that when I first wrote down this particular dream, of launching my own business, it must not have been in the divine plan for me to launch it immediately. Even though it was just my imagination then, it was also a dream for a future state of my life. But I admit that for years my lack of understanding of my purpose, my insecurities, my fears, my focus on present benefits rather than future payoffs, and my unwillingness to *decide* to jump out there and make it happen were more likely the reasons I procrastinated in doing the tasks needed to make this dream a reality sooner.

Examining My *Why*

When I started on my journey of understanding my purpose and drafting my life plan, I also began my journey of releasing the limits from my dreams. One of the first steps I took was to examine my *why*—not Why am I here? or Why am I wired this way? but Why is it that year after year I keep imagining the same dreams but putting off doing the tasks that will manifest them? Why am I not living my best life? and Why did it take me so long to find my purpose? This was a difficult conversation to have with myself, but it was necessary, and it was overdue. After all, I was now in my forties.

For years I had been going on an annual getaway where I would celebrate my successes, then write out my dreams and goals, only to go back home, put them in my nightstand, let them collect dust, and not make any of them a reality. I was proud of achieving a lot of goals and even patted myself on the back for many of my accomplishments, because celebrating successes are important, but these achievements were not tied to a larger purpose or aligned with a long-term strategy. The dreams I kept imagining were exciting, but I didn't have a *why* or a *so what* to tie them to.

After coming to understand the science of procrastination and the psychology of present bias, I realized that I kept putting my dreams on pause because the reality and the rewards were too far off and too expensive and required too much time and energy. These are common reasons that people procrastinate, many psychologists state. Other common reasons include feeling overwhelmed, perceiving lack of control, fearing failure, and seeking perfection. It wasn't until I crafted my purpose and vision statement and established my life plan that I was able to be more targeted in setting meaningful goals and to see all the pieces of the puzzle fit together. My goals were now taking me somewhere and giving me greater focus.

Prior to this, the goals I set were all well-meaning but fragmented and not aligned with any plan or strategy That is why I procrastinated. But the good news is that today I have achieved many of the dreams I wrote down years ago. Today I am working on new dreams. Today I understand why I procrastinated on certain things and am able to combat those reasons with the strategies I learned by going from being a *procrastinator* to being a *producer*.

Here is an example of the questions I asked myself in order to overcome procrastination:

- If I procrastinate, what will it cost me? If I get it done, what is the reward?
- Do I have the capacity, competence, and ability to do it?
- Am I passionate about this task?
- Are any guilt and shame driving my procrastination?
- Am I overwhelmed by the process of changing?
- If not now, when? If not me, who?
- What am I trying to avoid by not completing the task?
- How does putting off this task or decision make me feel?

Moving from Being a Procrastinator to Being a Producer

After challenging myself with those questions, I took a few other steps to move from being a procrastinator to being a producer. I revisited my life plan and refreshed my dreams and goals to ensure that they were aligned with each other. I prioritized them according to importance and made sure they were SMART goals. I first learned about SMART goals early in my career, in the 1990s, while studying management and later when attending a Management by Objectives seminar. This concept was first coined and developed by Peter Drucker and is still in common use. SMART goals are *specific, measurable, achievable, realistic,* and *time-bound.* This approach allowed me to stay focused on taking meaningful steps toward my dreams.

Next I listed all of the reasons I procrastinated on the tasks that were necessary to achieve my goals, such as fear, insecurity, lack of support, focus on the present, distractions, insufficient funds, and perfectionism. Yes, that's me: always needing things to be perfect, and when I didn't think they were I'd put off the task.

I then assessed what procrastinating had cost me, including the missed and lost opportunities. I wrote out some strategies for responding every time I felt the temptation to procrastinate. I decided I would cut myself some slack on small things I put off as long as I got them done within a reasonable time. I stopped being so hard on myself when I did not work out three times a week or didn't do the laundry on Tuesday or return a call to a friend by Friday.

I also learned the art and value of saying no. I talk about this more in the next chapter, but it is quite liberating to take control of what you take on. I am in the camp that believes that if a job is not worth doing well, then it's not worth doing at all. Sometimes we obligate ourselves to finish tasks we should not have taken on in the first place. In such situations, procrastination may be a form of passive-aggressively saying no. Rather than using passive-aggressive behavior, feeling frustrated, and living with regret, we can use assertive behavior by simply saying no, staying true to our priorities, and staying in our lane.

Learning a technique used by psychologists called *behavioral chaining*[5] helped me tremendously when I had procrastinated for so long I needed a jump-start. Chaining is an instructional strategy grounded in applied behavior analysis theory. It is based on task analysis, in which individual steps are recognized as requirements for task mastery. Chaining breaks a task down into small steps, then teaches each step in the sequence by itself.

When I considered a goal to be too lofty or complex, I would break up the bigger tasks and those tied directly to my dreams into smaller, more manageable parts. That way they didn't feel so overwhelming and cause me to hyperventilate at the thought of trying to tackle them. Using this method I would start with what are called *leading tasks*—tasks that are quick and easy and don't require much thought. For example, one of my goals was to get out of debt, but it was overwhelming to look at multiple large credit card balances and high interest rates and know where to start. Additionally, I had student loans, a car loan, personal loans, and a time-share bill.

My first leading task in the chaining method was to identify the credit card with the smallest balance and the highest interest rate. I paid off one credit card at a time rather than trying to tackle $22,000 all at once. My next leading task was to set up automatic bill pay on my bank account so that payments were sent directly to the credit card company instead of me procrastinating on mailing a check. Within six months the card was paid off, which boosted my confidence and increased my commitment. I then tackled the next lowest balance credit card with the next lowest rate of interest. The money I was no longer paying to the first credit card company was added to this payment, making it more than the minimum required payment. Using this technique of breaking down my goals into manageable tasks taught me how to approach all of my bigger dreams and goals, such as launching a business, and writing a book.

For years my dream was to write a book. I used to procrastinate because it felt like such a huge time commitment to sit down and do it. But when I broke it up into smaller tasks and committed to completing a few pages or a chapter at a time, it felt much more doable. I also learned that I didn't have to be confined to only one way of writing. Multiple methodologies and courses were out there for how to write a first book. They all taught me how to sit down and write it, but none of them gave me the revelation I got one day while talking to a friend, from whom I learned that audiobooks were becoming popular.

I learned that I didn't have to write my book, I could speak it. I enjoy speaking, and can do it with ease and knock it out pretty quickly from an outline, so a book suddenly felt doable and within my near future. I went into the studio and recorded it chapter by chapter over a few days, and finally it was done. So that's how I published my first book, *Reinvent Yourself.* It was an audiobook, but it was a book. I went from being a procrastinator to being the producer of my first book.

All those years I'd thought I had to have a hardcover book in hand, which seemed reasonable given that the Internet and social media were not as robust then as they are now. The dream of writing a book became a reality because I confronted the reasons I procrastinated; set realistic goals; broke them up into smaller, more manageable tasks; learned how to think outside the box and found a creative way that worked for me; and thus removed the limitations I had placed on myself. I later had the audiobook transcribed into a manuscript and published it as a hardcover book.

Another step I recommend to overcome procrastination and become more productive is to check in on your goals consistently (I do it at least monthly) to ensure you are staying on track. This is an important step that I can't stress enough. You have to adjust your goals as needed, because life happens and unexpected disruptions come that may require you to shift your timeline for completion.

An additional step is to identify a few trusted friends who will hold you accountable. Tell them your goal or dream and when you plan to accomplish it, and allow them to check in on your progress. Celebrate your milestones along the way. And when you feel the tendency to procrastinate, consider the consequences you may suffer, as well as the benefits and rewards you could gain. Call one of your trusted friends/accountability partners and talk about it, count to ten before you give in to the temptation, and revisit your journal of dreams and recommit to getting it done.

Procrastination may be the number one reason that most people don't realize their dreams, but science and psychology help us to understand why we do it. The good news is that procrastination is not a static condition. It comes down to deciding, committing, and acting. It's a daily fight and it's not easy, but we have the power to move from being a procrastinator to being a producer. When we release the limitations of procrastination, a world opens up that produces new possibilities, new opportunities, and new strategies for realizing our dreams.

Chapter 3

STUCK ON "WHAT IF?" COMMON DISEMPOWERING QUESTIONS

We all have an inner critic. That's not a surprise. What is surprising is the degree to which we entertain negative thoughts and allow them to inform our decisions, attitudes, and actions. Negative thoughts and self-doubt breed negativity. The more you put yourself down, the harder it will be to climb up. Self-talk isn't just idle noise. It reflects not only the way we think but also how we feel and act. We create our own reality by the words we speak. Telling ourselves we can do something can cause it to happen. Telling ourselves we can't do something can make it a reality. It's been said that the only things keeping us from getting what we want are the messages we keep telling ourselves and those that we keep believing.

It's my opinion that we are the sum total of all our thoughts, beliefs, and confessions. If we are serious about releasing the limits that keep us from realizing our dreams, we must start by exposing the questions that come from the negative thoughts, stories, and self-talk that we believe about ourselves. These *disempowering beliefs* can form at an early age, often developed from our experiences and internalized. They can lead to hopelessness, powerlessness, and worthlessness.

If we are honest, we can admit that we have all allowed disempowering beliefs to hijack our opportunities and leave us feeling one or more of these three emotions. There may have been jobs we didn't apply for, trips we didn't take, ideas we didn't share, or leadership roles we passed up because we were afraid they wouldn't work out, we might fail, we wouldn't be taken seriously, we might be rejected, and so on. We may have talked ourselves out of taking on these opportunities because we allowed the proverbial "What If?" questions to derail our purpose, our passion, and our possibilities.

The Start of My Disempowering "What If?" Beliefs

My First Pageant Competition

In chapter 1 I shared some of the dreams and imaginings I had as a child and how several of them became reality in my teenage years, building up my confidence and faith that anything I imagined was possible. One of those dreams was to compete in pageants and win a national title such as Miss America, Miss USA, or the like. You may recall that at the age of fourteen I competed in my first pageant, placed second runner-up, won the speech competition, and received positive feedback from the judges on my interview. But let me share with you the journey between my decision to compete and the final outcome. The days, weeks, and months leading up to it were wrought with second-guessing myself, feeling intimidated, and constantly having to be talked out of dropping out.

After completing the initial application and being accepted as a contestant, I was excited and couldn't stop talking about it. But as the pageant drew closer I met other contestants at the orientation meetings, then started to doubt myself. I was new to this arena, had never competed in pageants before, was only five feet tall, and was one of only three other minorities in the room out of nearly forty contestants. Most of them were tall, beautiful, blue- and green-eyed blondes. They touted their expensive gowns, that they had their own pageant coaches, and how many pageants they had competed in (and won). Others were buddy-buddy and knew each other from previous pageants. I started an internal conversation with myself, asking, "What are you doing here? What if you blow the interview and it is 50 percent of the scoring? What if you trip and fall in your gown? As a matter of fact, you can't afford an expensive gown, or a personal pageant coach. What if you botch the on-stage interview question? You are out of your league and your parents are not rich. Besides, you are the shortest one in the pageant *and* a newcomer. You don't stand a chance."

How many disempowering beliefs and questions did you count? Yes, this was a lengthy conversation I had with myself, and weeks after orientation I kept having that same conversation, and adding more reasons for quitting to the list. I looked at all of the downside and none of the upside. But each time I would talk to the pageant director and to my mom, and I would feel a little better and they would talk me into staying in the pageant.

Being Chosen as a Token

My career was not off-limits to these defining and disempowering beliefs. One of the most demoralizing experiences I suffered on a job was at a large retail sales company I loved working for. I was responsible for training all of the newly hired people managers. No matter their level or location, they were required to go through a five-day leadership training program within their first two weeks. One particular class included the new senior vice president (SVP) of human resources, to whom our department would ultimately report. Everything went great and he provided very positive feedback on the program. A few weeks later, his executive assistant called to schedule a meeting with the SVP and me. As you can imagine, I was both flattered and flustered at the same time. I wasn't sure of the nature of the meeting, and he was new to the company, so I didn't have a point of reference or know what to expect. But my supervisor assured me that the SVP was impressed with my experience and she had shared with him how valuable I was to the team.

In the meeting a few days later he complimented the course and confirmed what my supervisor had shared—that he was impressed with my skills and experience and wanted to make me a proposition. He went on to indicate that he was building his team and wanted me to be a part of it. He stated that he did not yet have a job title or a job description, and the position would not be posted for general staff to apply because he was offering it only to me. He said that for now he would say that I was assigned to Special Projects, and I would report directly to him. When I inquired what he envisioned the role doing, he responded, "We'll make it up as we go and as needs arise." I didn't know how to respond with anything other than OK. I didn't want to ask too many questions and appear to be difficult, so I thanked him for the opportunity and left his office feeling honored and confused at the same time. I didn't know if this position included a raise, how it would be announced to the organization, if I could share it with anyone yet, or what the transition would look like.

I certainly didn't feel like I could decline this offer, because it was presented not as an option but rather as a golden opportunity—a done deal— that I would be crazy to pass up. The SVP went on to state that he would work with my supervisor on setting a transition date to occur within a few weeks. Taking this job meant I would no longer be the leadership program trainer, and I would leave that location and my team members whom I had trained with and grown fond of for two years to move to the company's headquarters. After one meeting with the SVP my career was about to change and I had more questions than answers, but I also felt flattered and honored that I had been handpicked and offered the job.

When colleagues asked what I would be doing, I couldn't elaborate beyond working on special projects as assigned. A few weeks later I transitioned to the new role but still had no clear description of what was expected. On paper, HR listed me as a senior HR analyst, but I found out it didn't immediately include a raise or a promotion but was labeled as a lateral move. Then my first "special assignment" came. I was asked to audit one of the underperforming departments that there were a lot of employee complaints about. I had never done this type of assignment before, neither had I worked with this group of employees, nor had a formal announcement of my role ever been made. When I showed up at the department requesting documents and conducting focus groups to uncover issues and problems, you can imagine how I was received. I could have cut the tension with a knife and the rolling of eyes was not subtle. In a short time it spread across the organization that Shirley was the new SVP's spy. Certain staff asked what I did to get the job—implying that I had done something nefarious or sexual to get such a position. Behind my back I was called "John's girl" (that wasn't his name but you get the point). People asked why the position was not posted and what my "real job" was.

This went on for months, and defending my position became tiresome and all too common. The special assignments did feel like the role of a spy and an inspector. I wasn't enjoying this kind of work and I felt alone. But what could I do? I was stuck between a rock and a hard place because I knew I couldn't ask to go back to the leadership training role after only six months in the position. My previous role had been backfilled. Besides, I might upset the SVP who had handpicked me to work in his office, and I could be blackballed. It would be hard to live down being known as "John's girl."

I had no other choice but to search outside the company for new opportunities. Within weeks of applying for a position at a financial services firm ten minutes down the street, I got called for an interview for a senior HR consultant position. Training and development, which I loved to do, were a key part of the role. After several interviews, an extensive background and reference check, and passing the assessments, I was offered the job, which paid more than $20,000 more than I was making at the retail sales company. Plus, I knew what my responsibilities would include. I applied for a position that was legitimate, and this one was a perfect fit for my skills and experience, plus I didn't have to relocate and uproot my daughter. I was thrilled and relieved and couldn't wait to get out of the bad situation I was in.

The day after accepting the offer, I typed up my resignation letter and set up a meeting with the SVP of HR to tell him the good/bad news. I didn't know how he would respond. He had expressed such positive feedback about me when he called me into his office and offered me the position. I thought he might be disappointed, but I could never have imagined what actually happened that day.

I walked into his office but didn't give him the resignation letter immediately. I started the conversation by thanking him for the wonderful opportunity to be selected as part of his team. I went on to share the things I had learned on the projects I had worked on and thanked him for what I had learned. Then I told him I had just accepted a new position with the financial services firm down the street, that I would be doing something much more closely aligned with my talents and skill sets in training and development, and that it came with a huge raise.

As I told him I was submitting my two weeks resignation, I handed him the resignation letter. He threw it down without reading one word. His whole countenance changed. He turned two shades of dark red and with one finger pointed at my face. From across the desk he said, "You are so ungrateful. I cannot believe you would do this. I gave you a chance and you have blown it for every other Black person coming after you. I will never do this again. I don't need your two-week notice because today is your last day. Now get out of my office."

In an instant it felt like the world went silent and dark. It was as though everything moved in slow motion. I was in shock and disbelief. I didn't know how to respond. As I turned around to walk out of his office, I took a deep breath to keep from bursting into tears. When I left his office I went to the nearest restroom down the hall and ran into a stall. There the tears poured.

A few months after leaving the retail sales company, I found out that they had recently and quietly settled a multimillion-dollar race discrimination class action lawsuit during the same period in which I was approached with this offer by the SVP. I couldn't help but think that I had been singled out simply because of my race/ethnicity—as a token—and not because of my skills and experience. You can imagine how many disempowering "What If?" questions and beliefs came from this experience. I internalized every feeling from dejection, humiliation, and anger to hurt, rage, and fear. I even felt regret that I had not declined the SVP's offer or insisted on more details prior to accepting it; that I had not asked more obvious questions but rather had retreated and acquiesced to the offer that was doomed to fail because of how it circumvented the posting process.

The Person I Trained Became My Boss

Another devastating experience in my career that contributed to my disempowering beliefs about my value and self-worth occurred when I was on a steady trajectory toward being promoted to a senior level role in the organization I worked for. My boss at the time had identified me as "a high performer and a high-potential employee" because I had achieved the rating of 5 (the highest on a scale of 1 to 5) on my annual performance review for two consecutive years. He had also placed me on the company's succession plan and on an accelerated development plan to be considered for a senior leadership role within the next two to three years. Unfortunately he left the company before this process was complete. We had such a great rapport and I felt supported and championed, so it was a tremendous loss for me and I was left with a great deal of uncertainty about my role.

In the meantime, a woman I had worked with on other projects and trained on some of the new systems, procedures, and programs we had developed was promoted into my boss's job. She had very little experience working in our functional area and had worked with a much smaller team than mine, so I wanted to be sure I was clear about what her expectations of me were, and I didn't want to lose traction on the path I was on.

I met with her and shared my previous performance reviews, the feedback I had received from clients, and my aspirations for the next career level. I asked about her specific expectations of me. I wanted to ensure she would support my development. We discussed my goals, my performance objectives, and what success would look like. I even asked her what "exceeding expectations" and "absolutely stellar performance" would look like. I needed her to be specific about what "meeting expectations" was and about what "outstanding" was because I didn't want to start over simply because she was new in her role.

We sat down and laid those things out and agreed on what success would like. Once I had those specifics, I continued to work hard to exceed them. I was not given any feedback or any coaching from her, and you know if you haven't heard anything different you assume you're on track and that things are fine. But that December, at the end of the performance period, I was told that not only had I not "exceeded" expectations as I thought, but I wasn't even "meeting" expectations. You can imagine my reaction. When pressed about the ratings, she could provide no specific examples nor point to any impacts on the many clients I served, thus her ratings could not be substantiated. I had received an "exceeds expectations" for the past three years and now it had dropped two ratings in one performance cycle, with no justification.

It was one of the most hurtful experiences I have had in my career. I was highly effective at what I did—a great people leader according to my team and others. I knew how to run my department and my division, I gained great respect and support from my customers, and I achieved solid results beyond what was expected. I had received clear expectations and goals for the previous three years before her arrival, and I had worked hard. Now this person had come in and marginalized and sabotaged all that I had worked for. Yes, I felt angry, minimized, degraded, and betrayed, and it was my last straw.

In this instance, I went above her head. I involved HR and presented my case that before this person had come on as my supervisor, there had been three years of performance reviews in which I had always been rated very high, in which I could show that I was "exceeding" expectations. I asked what I could have done differently that warranted a lower rating, particularly because I'd never gotten any feedback to the contrary; she'd never provided any particulars. So HR requested that she rewrite the appraisal and change the ratings to match the performance. Turns out she did not want to give me credit for a lot of the results and successes in our division, because she had taken the credit in her own performance review.

Even though she attempted to revise the appraisal, it still wasn't to my full satisfaction. She watered down my results and worked even harder to unravel and sabotage the positive reputation I had built with my clients and in my division. Ultimately I moved on to a new role in another company, but that experience left a terrible stain on my confidence, my abilities, and my trust in leadership. It left me feeling like I had to work ten times harder just to get recognized, and to document everything I did so that I had extra proof of my performance. Even when I was deserving of a seat at the table, I often felt like I wasn't welcome or that I was tolerated when I was there. I felt like I had to overcompensate to get people to overlook my gender and my race. Ever been there? It is indeed and unfortunately why I pursued my Ph.D.

Why I Pursued My Ph.D.

I can't tell you the number of times throughout my career I asked my supervisor what it would take to get promoted or to move to the next level. I did a great job, as indicated on my performance reviews. I had the requisite skills. I achieved the results and got exemplary reviews from clients and colleagues. But most of my supervisors did not reward my performance beyond an occasional pat on the back and a measly yearly merit increase of 2 percent.

At various employers and in several positions I kept asking, "What would it take to get promoted?" only to get the typical runaround response of "Go take a course" or "Go through that certificate program" or "Get a mentor/coach" or "When you work on these kinds of projects and get that kind of experience, then you'll be ready." It was like a carrot being dangled in front of me and it consistently kept moving the closer I got to it. Even when I would move toward it and think I was about to grab it, it would move again. Those experiences were really disappointing, especially when I saw my male counterparts and nonminority colleagues getting promoted or selected for roles I knew they were less qualified for, and they didn't have to jump through any of the hoops I just listed.

So I went back to school and earned my master's degree. I got certifications in HR, employment law, training design, diversity, and inclusion. You name it, I earned it. I attended Darden's School of Business and earned a certificate in change management. I completed Harvard Business School's Executive Education program. I read books, secured a mentor, completed several Six Sigma courses, and went to more training programs than I can count. Ultimately I earned my Ph.D. in business and organizational leadership. I did this so that I could take away the excuses that were constantly being used to minimize my qualifications, even though I was already more qualified than some of them being promoted over me.

I also earned my Ph.D. so that I could position myself to gain the instant credibility, respect, and validation that the letters carry. I did it so that I would be among the top 2 percent in the world with those three letters after their name. Finally, I did it to set a standard for my daughter and to make my parents proud again. And they were.

Earning my Ph.D. allowed me to build an expansive list of skills and experiences on my resume; it positioned me as a global thought leader on HR topics and afforded me better career opportunities that paid more money. Unfortunately, the biases and discrimination didn't go away just because I earned a doctorate degree and attained more training. I still faced the realities of inequities and the imbalances of opportunities that exist in our society simply due to being a minority. And I still had to face the effects and questions that came from years of being marginalized, trivialized, overlooked, and undervalued.

In all of the stories I have shared here and in previous chapters, I had many disempowering conversations and developed a number of disempowering beliefs that started in my teenage years and followed me into my adult life. And with each new opportunity, new disempowering beliefs and questions presented themselves.

Whether talking myself out of participating in a pageant because I was out of my league, not trying out for a sports team because I might not get picked, not asking my boss for a raise I knew I deserved because I thought he/she would say no and label me ungrateful, not asking important questions that would help me make the best decision because I feared being perceived as challenging authority, avoiding speaking up and defending myself when I was publicly berated because I didn't want to lose my job, closing my heart off to getting involved with a man because I was afraid I would get my heart broken again, or not taking a risk simply because of being afraid of failing—the list goes on—these kinds of disempowering beliefs unfortunately talked me out of taking on some new projects, new opportunities, new jobs, and new relationships, and ultimately out of pursuing some of my dreams.

I know I am not alone; these beliefs are common to many. The examples I just shared are questions that occur not only in our personal lives but at work as well. Not addressing "What If?" questions in a timely manner can even derail an organization's success. I have found that they are one of the main reasons that so many change efforts fail. When leaders don't spend the time to address the staff's questions (which are often due to lack of understanding, not wanting to lose something, or fear of the unknown), change is made even harder. Their most common questions, which I have also asked, include, What if I lose my job? What if I get a cut in pay? What if I end working for a boss I don't like? What if I have to move? What if I fail? These are all legitimate questions, and when leaders address them they can provide stability and calm in the midst of change.

Following is a list of common disempowering "What If?" questions. Some I have just covered in my own stories. Others came from the many people I surveyed in my network. A few more came from people I interviewed for this book. As you review the list, assess which of these you keep believing and speaking to yourself. If you are the leader of a team, department, or company, consider which of these questions resonate in your role and which may come from your team members.

Disempowering "What If?" Questions

- What if I'm not good enough?
- What if I'm not attractive enough?
- What if I don't have enough money?
- What if I'm not smart enough?
- What if I get rejected or not selected?
- What if I get fired?
- What if I fail?
- What if I say the wrong thing?
- What if I am not qualified?
- What if I don't have time?
- What if I look stupid?
- What if my heart gets broken?
- What if others won't like me?
- What if I'm too old (or too young)?
- What if I succeed? Then what?

As you can see, these disempowering beliefs cover your career, business affairs, finances, relationships, health, and self-worth, and all of them are rooted in fear. (I share more about fear in the next chapter.) How long you have internalized these beliefs determines how much work you will need to put into dismantling them.

After recognizing that you have likely asked yourself one or more of these disempowering questions, you must then learn to take control of your destiny by transforming your thoughts into empowering beliefs. Empowering beliefs are those that inspire and push you to achieve what you want out of life. They give you confidence to succeed and to search for opportunities for growth and improvement.

Adrean Turner's story illustrates this concept perfectly. I was thrilled to interview her and to learn how she had been pushed into her purpose by replacing her old thoughts and beliefs with new knowledge and confessions. This push enabled her to "flip the script" on her "What if?" questions.

Adrean's Story

"PUSHED INTO PURPOSE"

More than a decade ago, Adrean embarked on a journey of spiritual renewal and self-discovery by revisiting the dreams she'd had as a young girl. Adrean was a married, full-time working mother of three small children. She was climbing the corporate ladder. But as her family grew and her career excelled, Adrean felt that something was missing from her life. She was not satisfied. She remarks, "Although my personal and professional success was rewarding, I knew there was more in life that I wanted to do and experience. I wasn't living my best life, and I knew there was more for me to do."

Having been through so much since those early dreams, she too was faced with questioning whether her dreams could actually become reality. At the same time, she was growing anxious that she had not fulfilled a particular dream that continued to follow her—starting her own business. She also dreamed of writing a book, but life seemed to always get in the way and derail her dreams, so she would go back to business and life as usual.

As she contemplated pursuing her dreams again, she found herself asking the same kinds of questions I have outlined in this chapter: What if I don't take this chance to pursue my dreams of owning my own business? What if I do launch it and fail again? What if I don't earn enough money? What if I lose my home over this? What if this drives a wedge in my marriage? Or worse, what if I can't do my part to take care of my family? Even though she knew she could always return to the workforce if she failed, she was still scared. She started losing hours of sleep at night envisioning being her own boss, but at the same time she was afraid—mainly because she wasn't sure what kind of business she wanted to start.

She researched multiple websites just trying to figure out what she wanted to do. And that's when she came across Les Brown. She listened to his motivational speeches and read his books, and her thinking began to shift from "What if?" to "When?" After internalizing his advice, Adrean got the push she needed and found out what her passion was— teaching, coaching, and training. She was pushed into her purpose. Within a year she walked away from a six-figure salary, benefits, stock options, and job stability to pursue her dreams. She still had one child in school and another one about to go to college, but she knew it was "now or never."

What a journey it was! While traveling the road of pursuing her dreams, Adrean encountered some peaks and valleys. She invested in a business venture that failed to get off the ground. She lost money, confidence, and time. She also encountered a number of other personal challenges that she didn't have time to recount in our interview.

As a result, Adrean had to put her dream on hold and reenter the workforce full-time in temporary positions so she could recoup her financial loss and keep her family afloat. But she was determined not to give up. In her spare time she launched an online talk show and began a career in teaching to supplement her income. Eventually her hard work and determination paid off; a few years later she launched Turner Coaching, Training and Consulting, LLC. Today, after working in corporate America for twenty-three years, Adrean is an award-winning certified coach, author, empowerment speaker, professional development trainer, podcast host, and business consultant. She is also the author of the book *Fearless*.

Adrean admits she still faces those "What if?" questions when she feels stuck; but after going through her journey of self-discovery and spiritual renewal, she thinks and believes differently. Instead of dwelling on the negative aspects of her "What if?" questions, she has learned to "flip the script" and be more positive.

For example, a couple of months ago she was interested in investing the time and money in a program. The program was a bit costly, but it sounded like a great fit for where she wanted to go. Instead of entertaining the disempowering question, What if you invest in this training and it's not what you expected? she responded with an empowering statement: If I attend, I will feel more confident when speaking and presenting. I will learn new skills and techniques. I will enhance my brand, make new connections, and use the information to create a product to sell to clients. By responding to her "What if?" questions in this way, Adrean took back her power and nullified the temptations from her past that came to place limits on her dreams and her future.

During our interview, she expressed that she now feels more motivated and empowered to seize opportunities rather than run from them due to fear. She admitted that she is living her dreams today because she feels better equipped to make strategic decisions rather than emotional ones. Today Adrean Turner is living her dreams while pursuing new ones and is optimistic about her future.

Debunking/Dismantling Disempowering Beliefs

If you are asking, What if I'm not good enough? ask yourself next, Where is this feeling coming from? Why do I believe this? Also consider who it is that makes you feel less than good enough and why you are giving that person so much power over your self-worth. When I was told by my supervisors that I wasn't qualified for a position or promotion, or when they talked to me in a way that made me feel worthless and devalued, I had a choice to make. Sometimes I was caught off guard and allowed myself to have a pity party. Other times, as you heard in several of my stories in the previous chapters, I ignored their comments and talked to someone else who made me feel that I *was* valued. Yet other times I confronted the person and defended myself. Remember that each of us has something of value to offer and should not allow others to rob us of our uniqueness. It really comes down to having the right attitude and the right people around you, and making the right choices.

Instead of drowning in self-doubt, take inventory of your strengths and good traits and work on developing them and becoming better every day. Get healed of the disease I have called *comparisonitis* and measure your success in terms of your own purpose and goals. The only comparison you should make is between your past self and how you are evolving and getting better, wiser, and stronger from every experience.

If you are asking, What if I fail? welcome to the club. This was of my most common disempowering questions. What I've come to realize is that failure is a natural part of life and something every single one of us has experienced. I have failed in relationships, in leading projects, in making right decisions, and in business. But I have learned that some of the world's most successful people failed many times before they succeeded.

I'd like to challenge you to rethink a number of disempowering quotes. First, I have asked many people, What would you do if you knew you couldn't fail? The response is consistently, I would accomplish all the dreams I put on hold. Then they list all of them. But let's dissect the question a bit. The question implies that failure is bad and is the one thing that gets in the way of our realizing our dreams. What if we answered that question with a different perspective? What if the answer is, I would do nothing? Instead of eliminating the possibility of failure from our life, how about developing the right attitude toward failure? Think of it this way: failure is a part of the process of living. To live the life we've imagined, we must confront the fear of failure and even failure itself. What decides your future is what you choose to believe. Whether you believe that you will fail or that you will succeed, you're right.

Second, many of us may have been taught that failure is not an option. As I have grown through challenges, mistakes, and failures, I have come to believe that had I not failed at something I would not have learned anything. Failure can be an option as long as we recognize that failure isn't final, that it isn't forever. Leadership expert and best-selling author John Maxwell wrote a book called *Failing Forward* in which he tells us that it's OK to fail at something and to fall—we just need to "fall forward." This simply means that we need to learn from our failures, learn from our mistakes, and not be afraid to get back up and take our lives to the next level. Falling doesn't mean you've reached the end of the road. You can use it as a springboard to the next level of your life.

One of my mentors used to say, "If you fall down and you can look up, you can get up." There's an opportunity for all of us to learn from our mistakes, because we all make them. No one is exempt from failing, from making mistakes, from having hiccups in their life. But the difference between those who succeed and those who stay stuck is that those who succeed realize that failing is a natural part of the journey toward success. We must learn to deal with our fear of failure and not let it control us.

We must believe that anything worth having is worth fighting for and sometimes worth failing at. I would go on to compete in more than thirty pageants, and I lost more than I won, but I won the ones that counted. All of the losses were lessons I leveraged for the next pageant. Each loss taught me a new lesson and each one made me a more formidable competitor. There is no shame in failing; there is only shame in not accepting the challenge to keep trying. Grow from your failures and move on.

If you are thinking you don't have enough money to pursue your dream, do your homework. It may not be the case at all. One of the reasons I avoided starting my business for years was because I thought it would require tens of thousands of dollars up front. Maybe some business opportunities do, such as buying a franchise or opening a nightclub, day spa, boutique, or restaurant. But I wanted to open a consulting, training, and coaching business. I thought I would need to develop a $5,000 business plan and that getting a business license was a tedious and long-term process. I thought I would have to find office space, sign a long-term lease, spend a lot of money on office equipment, hire a full-time staff person, and do a lot of newspaper and radio advertising.

But after conducting some research, I found that I could operate my business initially from my home, that getting a business license took just a few days, and that the costs were minimal. I could get a post office box as a business address for a few hundred dollars a year, and business cards for under a hundred dollars; I could get a WordPress website developed for about two thousand dollars; and I could hire a virtual assistant for a few hours a week, all within my budget. For years I had operated under this

"What if?" question and assumed that running my own business was far out of my reach financially. It turned out that what held me back was my lack of information and understanding driven by fear and a sense of inadequacy. As a result, my dream was on hold for years, until I finally jumped. I talk more about that in chapter 7.

If after you do your homework you find that your business does require a lot of money up front, devise a plan. Start putting money aside for it each pay period; investigate resources and financing options through organizations such as the Small Business Administration and SCORE, your bank, and industry associations; and consider friends, colleagues, and family members as your initial investors. There are also a number of "startup pitch competitions," which will allow you to pitch your business idea to potential investors, with the best ideas winning financing.

What I learned after years of delaying my dream because I thought I couldn't afford it was that I didn't have to start out in grandiose style. I didn't have to start out with an expensive lease in an ivory tower. I could grow into a building on the basis of the business need. I didn't have to hire a bunch of people to get my business started; I could start with contract workers, friends, and a part-timer, then build up my staff to full-time as the business justified it. I didn't have to have an expansive and expensive marketing campaign, and I didn't have to have a $10,000 website to get started. I started out with word-of-mouth marketing, some social media announcements, and a WordPress website for $2,000.

Another "What if?" question that stifled my progress was, What if I get rejected or don't get selected? Even though I had dealt with this when trying out for sports teams and pageant competitions, in relationships, and when applying for jobs, I would still experience that sinking feeling and the impact that rejection had each time I was not selected, when someone told me no, or when the relationship didn't work out. None of us likes this feeling, and if we're not careful we can take it so personally that it paralyzes us from trying new things. I overcame this by learning how to shift my perspective to see that if and when I was rejected, the job, the relationship, the opportunity wasn't meant for me—and something or someone better or different was coming along. I began to believe that things happened for a reason, and even though we don't always understand why things happen, over time they have a way of working out a better outcome.

I remember getting turned down for a position that I thought for sure I should have been hired for. It paid very well and would have been a promotion for me. I met every qualification they listed and nailed all of the interviews. You know that feeling of pride and confidence you have when you've performed at your best, only to receive that dreaded rejection letter a week later that reads, "While your background and experience were impressive, we have decided to go in a different direction"? That's what I felt. But sometime later I was offered a better opportunity (more money, better benefits, and a better work environment). In other cases, when I was rejected I would find out later that things were not the way they were represented anyway, and it would not have been a good experience had I gotten the job.

I experienced this same thing with relationships that didn't work out. I have been married, I have been divorced, and I have been rejected and betrayed on a number of occasions by people I trusted, loved, and respected. I took these rejections a bit harder, of course, because they were more personal. There were times when I felt the rejection so deeply that I put up walls around my heart, making it hard to trust in the next relationship.

But after experiencing several heartbreaks, I came to understand a few realities. I had to be more selective about whom I chose to get involved with, and I couldn't allow someone else's indiscretions or character flaws to redefine the core of who I am. I rejected the temptation to be bitter, live in regret, and get vengeful, much as I wanted to, but I chose to get better, to forgive and move on, and to learn from the experience. As time passed, I consistently saw how much better I was without those kinds of people in my life. In chapter 6 I provide tips on the power of having the right relationships and on how they can contribute to your ability to realize your dreams.

So, the next time you ask the question, What if I get rejected? just know that it's not a bad thing, it's not always personal, and life has a way of giving us signs and symbols when some things are not meant to be. We just have to learn to read the signs and follow their direction.

I could share here so many more experiences of how I faced every one of these disempowering "What if?" questions, but you'll hear more in the following chapters. Know that for every disempowering question there is always an empowering response that you can use. If you are asking any of the following disempowering "What If?" questions, know that so did I. One of the exercises that became a ritual in my journey to get beyond my "What if?" questions was listing the most common disempowering questions that would keep me stuck and then countering them with some of the statements I would actually say to myself as affirmations. I invite you to start with three to focus on this week until your language changes. Then select three more empowering responses the following week, and three more the week after that, until you have identified and debunked every disempowering question that derails your destiny. Make a commitment to reprogram your mind to have an empowering response for every one of them. (See pages 58–59)

Overcoming our disempowering beliefs isn't easy. It takes a significant amount of work, introspection, and time. Moreover, it isn't a "one and done." You don't just go through this process once and be finished with it. Rather, it's an ongoing process of steps we must revisit over and over. We must therefore commit ourselves to long-term change, and our beliefs are of course at the core of that transformation. They are the foundation of who we are. Remember, the beliefs that got you to where you are today won't get you to where you want to be tomorrow. They influence every aspect of your life. Don't let your beliefs prevent you from living that life you've always imagined.

As I close this chapter about being stuck on "What if?" and the disempowering beliefs that can derail our dreams, I remember what Mahatma Gandhi said:

> Man often becomes what he believes himself to be. If you keep on saying to yourself that you cannot do a certain thing, it is possible that you may end by really becoming incapable of doing it. On the contrary, if you have the belief that you can do it, you can certainly acquire the capacity to do it even if you may not have it at the current moment.[1]

Our beliefs must change with the times; they must also change alongside our goals. If *they* don't change, then *we* don't change, and our dreams
will always remain on pause.

Disempowering "What If?" Questions	Empowering Responses
What if I'm not good enough?	I am unique and special. There is greatness inside of me and I have something of value to offer. I will give it my best and continue to grow. If someone doesn't think I'm good enough, it's only their opinion. Most important, it's about how I feel about me, and I AM good enough.
What if I don't have enough money?	This is a temporary state. Money is a resource, but it doesn't define who I am. I am on a financial management plan to save, increase my income, and one day finance my dreams.
What if I'm not smart enough?	What I don't know now I am open to learning. I am a lifelong learner who will continue to educate myself.
What if I get rejected or not selected?	Things happen for a reason. This was not the right opportunity or the right person, so a better one is around the corner. I won't stop trying because what one person may not see in me many more will.
What if I get fired?	I would be released to pursue new opportunities. Everything has an expiration date, so it must have been time to move on. When I ask or do something that is based on my personal conviction, I won't be afraid of the consequences. Better opportunities will come along.
What if I fail?	Failure is a part of life but it's not the end of the world. I will keep trying and I will learn from the experiences and be better the next time.

What if I am not qualified?	I have many gifts and talents that I can contribute. I am continuing to grow new skills that will enhance my qualifications. I am a person of value and I will find the right fit.
What if I don't have time?	Everyone has the same amount of time in a day and I will manage mine wisely. I will plan appropriately and learn to be a better steward of the time I have. I will learn to say no and learn to delegate when it's necessary, and I will not take on more than I can handle.
What if I look stupid?	I'm going to give it my best shot and be proud that I tried.
What if my heart gets broken?	Hearts can heal and I deserve to find love. I will keep my heart and mind open. If I had it broken before, I will forgive; I will not get bitter; I will get better. I cannot assume that the next person will break my heart; they may be the best thing to happen to me.
What if others don't like me?	I don't live by the approval of others. I am not trying to win a popularity contest. I have a great network of people around me who support and like me. If I don't have the right people around me, I will find them.
What if I'm too old or too young?	There's an old adage that says I am never too young to teach or too old to learn. I have so many lived experiences to share. I bring a fresh new perspective. I am open to learning new things.
What if I succeed? Then what?	I'll learn from the things that worked and from the things that didn't. I will celebrate my successes and continue to work hard. If I succeeded once, I'll succeed again.

Chapter 4

FACE YOUR FEARS HEAD ON

Where Does Fear Come From?

*D*id you know that we are born with only two fears? The fear of falling and the fear of a loud sound. All other fears are taught and acquired through experiences, associations, and what we are told. Some of the most common fears I've heard others share include fear of dying, fear of heights, fear of closed spaces, fear of public speaking, fear of taking risks, fear of the unknown, fear of failure, and fear of success—and that's just for starters. While fear is both a learned behavior and a part of human nature, oftentimes it's just a figment of our imagination, a negative anticipation, or a suspicion of what might happen in the future. In my faith, we define fear as False Evidence Appearing Real (FEAR), meaning that our mind can magnify anything we worry about and make it seem insurmountable even when it really is small. We also describe fear as being the opposite of faith.

Fears come from what we've been taught and experienced. If fear is a learned response, we can unlearn our fears and relearn a different response. My mentor Mr. Les Brown says, "We are either living our dreams or living our fears." Which one are you living?

Fear is an emotion that results from some real or imagined threat to our well-being. It diminishes our confidence, denies our potential, destroys our relationships, devalues our existence, and defers our dreams. It leaves us living in a state of complacency because we're afraid of the obstacles along the way or the outcomes at the end, or both. Before even starting we end up in a spiral of self-doubt and worry. A life lived constantly in fear will never move forward but instead will become more frustrated as time goes on, as we wonder if things would've been different if we had made some different decisions. This is where I lived for years. I call it living in a state of woulda, coulda, shoulda, and one day. Only when we acknowledge and admit to the fear can we take that first step forward toward releasing these limits.

Walking and living in fear can cause us to create what I call a Golden Cage around ourselves as a safety mechanism that protects us from the world but also blocks others out. If we stay in that cage too long, it gets comfortable and familiar. We can even start to accessorize our cage so that it looks and feels pretty and comfortable to live in. And even though we feel safe and the cage is all dressed up, we don't realize that we are isolating ourselves from others and creating self-imposed limitations that keep us from living our best life.

This was the case with a former coworker I'll call Stephanie. Due to the circumstances surrounding her story, I have chosen a different name to protect her identity. On the outside she had the perfect persona and everyone believed what she portrayed. No one knew that it was a facade, and by the time we found out it was too late.

Stephanie's Story

IT WAS ALL A FACADE

Stephanie and I became friends while working in the Training Department at a bank. She worked in Operations and I worked in Client Services. She was always upbeat, with a great attitude, and was extremely smart. All of the workers loved working with her, and she was one of the bank's most experienced and highly rated training specialists. When I left the bank for another job opportunity, we stayed in touch.

She had fallen in love with one of the bank's executives and gotten married, but within two years she went through a bitter divorce. When they first started dating it was quite the drama around the bank. He was a vice president in the Marketing and Analysis Department and it was against company policy to date within the company. Eventually an exception was made because they were not in the same division or location, but there were still a lot of rumors about the relationship and the potential implications.

When they got married, the rumors shifted to how Stephanie had hit the jackpot by marrying him—the big home they purchased (five bedrooms, four bathrooms, four thousand square feet), the new designer clothes she wore, and the new BMW he bought for her. She seemed to take it all in stride and seemed very happy, so I was happy for her.

When the marriage fell apart, he sold the home. Stephanie moved in with a friend and he relocated to a different state and began a new life. In essence, he dropped her like a hot potato and never looked back. She was left broken, devastated, and humiliated. As time passed, I began to see a change in Stephanie. A few times when we talked she confided in me that he had cheated on her several times, even while they were dating, and she always forgave him. She continued to act like everything was OK and even took the blame for his cheating.

Turns out he was also verbally abusive to her and made her feel like she was never good enough. Her dad was never in her life, so she looked up to him as a father figure (he was twelve years older). She feared being alone and abandoned and he took advantage of that, so she settled for whatever he dished out. Of course no one knew that all of this was going on, because they appeared as the perfect, happy couple at work.

A few months passed. Stephanie stopped returning phone calls and posting on her social media pages, which was unusual because she was always sharing poems, quotes, and links to pages she liked. Eventually she left that job and didn't tell anyone where she went, so we lost touch. She had shut us out and isolated herself from friends and coworkers, and it appeared she wanted it that way.

A few years later I learned that Stephanie had become addicted to prescription drugs as a result of depression and anxiety and ended up overdosing. How devastating it was to know that a friend with so much promise and passion for life, who made all of us smile with her bubbly personality, had allowed the vicissitudes of life to defeat her. She had created a Golden Cage that she had dressed up and made look pretty from the outside, then insulated herself in it, shutting out anyone who wanted to help her. She allowed her fears, the rejection, and the embarrassment of a failed relationship to overtake her will to live out her dreams, and ultimately her will to live her life.

Stephanie's story may be your story. Maybe it doesn't end the same way, but the feelings of failure, betrayal, hurt, and bitterness may be your current reality. Are you shutting yourself off from others who want to help you? Are you isolating yourself from reality because the pain of your past makes it too hard to face your future? Have you built a Golden Cage and accessorized it to be your comfort zone? Are you giving voice to those negative, self-defeating, life-limiting questions that could cause to you meet Stephanie's fate? Maybe you are still alive, just not living.

In the last chapter I detailed some of the most common disempowering "What if?" questions that cause us to abandon or avoid pursuing our dreams or new opportunities. I shared many of those that I experienced personally, which shaped and influenced the way I perceived myself. At the heart of my disempowering "What if?" questions was fear. For years I was living my fears and allowing my dreams to diminish. Fear can cause us not only to give up on our dreams but also to give up on living if we don't face them head on.

What do you fear? Why? How has it affected your dreams and your future? Are you willing to face your fears head on?

Facing My Own Fears

Because of fear, I stayed at jobs far beyond my expiration date. I was afraid to quit because I didn't know if the grass that looked greener on the other side was actually artificial turf. I've vacated many great ideas—ideas that could have impacted someone else's life but I talked myself out of them because of fear. I could have launched my own business a decade ago, and been successful, but I was afraid it would fail and I would be in more debt as a result.

I've even avoided getting involved in relationships because I was afraid they might be another abusive, toxic, or unhealthy situation. Fears I developed from experiences I had at an early age followed me into my adult life and impacted my decisions for years. Some of those fears were beyond my control; I didn't see them coming, nor could I have prevented them.

Developing My Fear of Deep Water

One such event happened when I was just thirteen years old. I was attending a pool party with my softball team at the home of one of our teammates. We had just won the championship game. We were celebrating and having a blast with lots of great food, music, and games in the backyard. As I was walking alongside the pool, someone pushed me in from behind and ran off. I never saw it coming, and before I knew it I was ten feet under water. I had not yet learned to swim, and no one knew that. After a few seconds I panicked and started fighting the water. Because everyone was playing and laughing, no one immediately noticed that I was struggling to get to the top. Moments later, after seeing my life flash in front of me and feeling even more panicked, I felt a hand grab my arm and push me up. Then someone pulled me to the side of the pool and others helped to lift me out. I emerged coughing, choking, shaking, and crying from so much fear. I never forgot that near death experience. OK, maybe I wasn't near death, but it felt like it to me. I saw my life flash before me. It put into my heart a paralyzing fear of deep water that I didn't have before this incident, and now, forty years later, as I write about it, I can still see it like it was yesterday.

The other experience that caused me to develop a fear I didn't have before was the story I shared in chapter 1 about being held at gunpoint during a bank robbery. That experience had a different effect on me than nearly drowning. As a result of that life-threatening and life-altering event,

I am still afraid of guns. I know it's been said that it's not guns that kill people, it's people that kill people, but having had one pointed directly at my head changed my perspective about them forever. I don't want to be in the same room with a gun, don't want one in the house, and don't want to learn to use one. Even when I've seen movies that have a violent bank robbery scene (such as *Set It Off, Inside Man, and Going in Style,* to name a few), I've been triggered and have remembered my experience all over again, like it was yesterday. On both of these occasions I experienced fear in such a significant and unforgettable way that they still affected me decades later. One of them I conquered (my fear of deep water), the other one I have learned to live with (fear of guns).

This is how we learn to fear. The experience may not be as traumatic and life altering as the two I have shared, but with fear there is always a reaction. Sometimes we are paralyzed or panicked from the fear. Sometimes we flee from fear, other times we avoid doing something because of fear. And sometimes we have to confront fear head on. I've been in all of these situations many times. Here are a few instances of how I conquered some of my deepest fears.

Facing My Fear of Deep Water

Until a few years ago, I was still deathly afraid of swimming in deep water. Every time I took swimming lessons and tried to conquer the fear, I would be overcome with the memory of drowning. And it was hard to trust that anyone who was teaching me to swim was not going to throw me into deep water and expect I would learn that way. It affected me so much that when my daughter was a baby I made sure she took swimming lessons so that she would never have the experience of being pushed into a pool and not knowing how to swim.

Here's how I finally conquered my fear of deep water. One year I was on a speaking tour in Barbados with a group of fellow speakers and friends. Everyone wanted to rent WaveRunners and go out into the ocean. Immediately I refused and told them I'd wait for them to return. I shared my story of why I was fearful, not to mention that I was also afraid of sharks from watching the movie *Jaws* and hearing of shark attacks. Several of my companions assured me that it was perfectly safe and a lot of fun, and we would be wearing life jackets. Two I was close to and trusted most responded that they would let me ride on the back of their WaveRunner. I paused to consider while they continued to assure me that it would be fine and that they were skilled at riding these vehicles. They also made the case that it was time for me to get over my fear, and what better way than with friends.

After much consternation and an interrogation of the WaveRunner rental agent about the safety of the vehicle, the death record of other riders in the past, and how often shark attacks occurred in Barbados, I reluctantly agreed, with the caveat that I would ride on the back with one of the friends who had offered. I put on my life jacket and off we went, out into the expansive ocean. We started out slow so that I would feel more comfortable. Then we sped up. After a few minutes I was enjoying it and agreed we could go even faster. At full speed we approached the turn to come back to the hotel. My friend did not slow down enough and as we took that turn, down went the WaveRunner into the water, throwing me out into the deep. Immediately fear gripped me, and all I could think was that I would drown or that a shark was nearby about to attack. But within milliseconds I calmed myself and remembered what the WaveRunner agent had said in response to all of my questions: "In case of an emergency or if you fall into the water, don't panic, stay calm. Your life vest will cause you to float to the top." He had also told me I didn't have to worry about shark attacks there.

This time I didn't fight the water like I did when I was younger, and I didn't panic. I talked to myself and stayed calm. Within those milliseconds I felt my body rise to the top (not fast enough for me), and when my head came above the water, I could see my friend get back on the WaveRunner, immediately come to me, grab my hand tight, and help me get back on. I didn't have a choice but to get back on, and this was a good thing because it forced me to confront my fear from the previous experience in the midst of facing fear in my current situation. Yes, I was terrified at first, but I caught myself and remembered what to do, and it turned out OK. We rode back much slower, but I was OK. I was glad I had asked the rental agent a lot of questions about what to do, and that I was with people

I trusted who knew what to do. It helped me to face my fear. The next day I went back out again, riding on the back of the WaveRunner with another friend, and we did not fall. We had a blast. More important, that trip was a turning point for me in facing my fear of deep water.

Facing My Fear of a Bully

A bully tormented me throughout my high school years. I was petite, weighing only 90 pounds, and she was much taller than me. All of my classmates were afraid of her, but I knew I couldn't cower when she threatened to beat me up. If I did, she would increase her attacks and all of my friends would make fun of me.

In our 12th grade year, near the end of third semester, she announced to the class that she would meet me at my bus stop after school and beat me up. Of course that generated a lot of spectators who normally didn't take my bus route from school. The bus stop was a few houses down from where I lived. Fortunately my bus arrived a few minutes before hers. I got off and ran into the house. As much as I wanted to hide and pretend that I wasn't home, I knew I had to confront my fear and defend myself. And that I did. Her bus arrived a few minutes later and she and the crowd walked to my house. Someone yelled my name and announced that she was outside and that I should come out and get my butt whooping. I had changed my clothes and shoes and prepared myself for the fight. I walked outside and into the street, where she was, and as soon as she hastened toward me I threw the first punch. Some called it a haymaker, but I kept throwing them, mostly out of fear that if I stopped she would hurt me worse. It turns out they had to pull me off her. I had won the fight.

The next day at school, all of my classmates were calling me Sugar Ray Leonard (an American welterweight boxing champion from the 1980s). Because I defended myself, the bully left me alone, and I sent a message to others that I wasn't afraid and they shouldn't mess with me. The truth is, I was still afraid of the bully even after the fight, but I felt a sense of pride and relief that I had faced my fear of her, and discovered I had a pretty nice right hook.

I learned a few lessons from that incident that followed me into my adult life. First, when I was fearful, I didn't realize my own strength until I had to come face to face with my insecurities and inadequacies. Second, had I not stood up to that fear (the bully), the torment would have continued. In other words, you cannot conquer what you aren't willing to confront. Third, when faced with fear, it may not be as big and as bad as it appears. It may just be sounding off a lot of noise but not be able to overtake you.

Facing My Fear of Dentists

Another lingering fear I had to face was going to the dentist. Oh, how I dreaded even the thought of making an appointment. As a result I would procrastinate or reschedule. Many years ago I had to undergo a root canal, and on another occasion I had to have a tooth extracted. On both occasions I lived a nightmare. The dentist who pulled my tooth was rude, demonstrated no empathy, and after an hour of drilling and handling my mouth really roughly, told me he couldn't get the tooth out and would have to refer me to a specialist. I developed not only a fear of dentists but also a disdain for them. Years later I had an abscess and was in a lot of pain. Remembering what I had endured from the previous dentist, I knew I had to confront my fear.

First, I sought out referrals from friends who'd had great experiences with their dentist. Second, I read those dentists' Google reviews to confirm that they were highly rated by others. Third, I asked the dentist I picked a lot of questions in order to get a lot of assurances before scheduling the procedure. Ultimately, it turned out to be the best experience I had ever had with a dentist. She was very nice and gentle, talked me through every step, and checked to see how I was feeling and if something was hurting too much, and her soothing voice made all the difference. Later that evening she called and checked on me to ensure that I was recovering OK. Ever since then my fear of dentists has diminished substantially. Today I am pleased to report that I have been using that dentist for the past four years and have no more fear. Her amazing "bedside manner" continued and made all the difference for me. I have even referred her to several others who also were afraid of dentists.

Throughout my life there have been many other fears that I have faced head on. I have confronted friends, family, and partners who betrayed or abused me and made me feel small, insecure, and afraid to say anything. I have confronted bad bosses who belittled and berated me in front of others and made me feel powerless and undervalued. I've also learned that some fears don't go away and you have to learn to live with them, such as my fear of guns. I also learned that some fears may go away but also return, such as my fear of failing and my fear of getting hurt. But you have to learn to confront them again and again, sometimes with a different strategy. Some fears are stronger than others and some I am still working on overcoming, but at least I have conquered most of the fears that paralyzed me and kept me from realizing my dreams.

Six Steps for Facing Your Fears Head On

I have shared my truth about living with a lot of fears and how I faced them. Here is a summary of the steps I took and some lessons I learned by doing so.

First, I shifted my thinking and my attitude about my fears by acknowledging them. I learned that what you resist will persist, and that you cannot conquer what you are not willing to confront. I recognized that fears are a normal part of life and all of us have them.

When I took on another job or decided to leave a bad relationship, I wrote down every bad thing that could happen, then listed how they would affect me. Beside every fear I listed some strategies for how to respond. Doing this exercise took the power out of the fears I had, and I felt more in control. Turns out that most of the things I worried about never happened anyway.

Second, I asked a lot of questions and sought to dismantle my fears by seeking reassurances like I did in the story of getting on the WaveRunner or finding a new dentist. When I was considering a new job assignment, I sought out people who had been in the role prior to me and asked them a lot of questions so I could understand what I was getting into. I took the same approach in dating relationships as well—asking a lot of questions. Sometimes it turned the prospect off, other times it was a welcome exercise for getting to know each other.

Third, I jumped out there and gave it a try. I decided not to be paralyzed by fear, whether fear of failure, fear of drowning, fear of getting hurt, fear of getting beat up, and all of the fears listed in the previous chapter. I faced one fear at a time. I didn't overwhelm myself by trying to conquer too much too fast. I took baby steps, but I did step out. And when I faltered, I immediately tried again before fear set back in.

Fourth, I built up my self-confidence and sense of self-worth by speaking positive and empowering affirmations. There is power in our words and we can use them to build up instead of tear down. When I felt fear, I chose to calm down and not panic. I remembered what others who were more experienced told me to do, and then did it.

Fifth, when I conquered a fear, I wrote down what I did and used it as a testimonial to recall for the next fear I faced.

Last, I continued to imagine my dreams becoming reality. I learned to see myself beyond my fear and to think of the best-case scenario instead of dwelling on the worst-case scenario. These six steps helped me to release the limits I had placed on myself.

Think of the fears you need to face. Consider how they have affected your life and the decisions you've made. More important, think about how they have kept you from seizing opportunities and realizing your dreams. Remember, we are either living our fears or living our dreams. Fear is the single biggest limitation that holds us back and causes us to procrastinate, make excuses, and stay stuck. But fear doesn't have any special power other than that which we give it. That means we also have the power to release fear and begin living beyond "What if?"

PART 2

Realize Your Dreams

Chapter 5

IN SEARCH OF SIGNIFICANCE

*I*n part 1 of this book you learned about the numerous self-imposed limitations that I allowed to control more than half of my life and how they affected my thinking, believing, and ultimately my actions. In chapter 1 I revealed that early in my childhood my dreams were unhindered and that I experienced the manifestation of several of them before I went off to college. This gave me great confidence and a feeling that nothing was impossible to achieve. I was in my early twenties when I experienced my first significant failures, hurts, near-death experiences, divorce, financial ruin, emotional breakdown, and shattered dreams. Life's twists, turns, and tests caused my self-confidence to be weakened, my fears to be strengthened, my faith to be diminished, and my dreams to be delayed. And they would stay that way until I did some in-depth personal work and recovery.

That recovery started with working through the reasons I procrastinated and the necessary steps I needed to take to become a producer rather than a procrastinator (chapter 2). Next I had to expose all of the disempowering "What if?" questions that I had allowed to flood my psyche and infect my belief system (chapter 3). The work continued with identifying the many fears I had developed from these life experiences and how I had to confront them head on (chapter 4). Doing this work took years of focus, commitment, and facing unpleasant realities about myself, but it got me away from a very dark place and put me on a positive path where my search for significance began.

In part 2 I continue my journey beyond releasing the limits and describe the long and difficult road I traveled to realize my dreams after many years of tears. In this chapter, I share how I reimagined my life by identifying my *why* and establishing my life plan. I also detail the importance of fostering the right relationships, starting with self (chapter 6), and of building the courage to take risks so that you can jump to your destiny (chapter 7). Part 2 is chock-full of steps, strategies, and tactics that I employed to get to where I am today, and of the many payoffs of living beyond "What if?" (chapter 8). I continue to share not only my own stories but also those of others who faced some of the same battles I did, confronted them, and as a result have realized their dreams too.

Beginning a New Ritual—Annual ME-TREATS

After having so many life-changing experiences in the span of a decade, I found myself again in search of significance—having to reset, reinvent myself, and find new meaning for my life. So I started a new ritual. At the end of every year, in December, I would celebrate the Christmas holidays with my family, then leave my daughter with my parents or with her other set of grandparents and race off to the airport to catch my flight. I'd use the annual bonus money that my employer gave to its employees when they had a profitable year and head to the Caribbean or another tropical island. For five to seven days I would spend time alone. It was a time of retreating, refreshing, resting, and refueling after a long, demanding, hectic, and draining year. I started calling this yearly ritual my ME-TREAT.

My job at the time required me to travel quite a bit. I was managing a large department and leading a large team. I was a single mom with a very active adolescent, I was in school earning my master's degree, and I didn't take much vacation time throughout each year—a day here and a few days there, but not a full week. So, when the end of the year came, you can imagine how ready I was to take a break from work, school, home responsibilities, and yes, even mommy duties. Bermuda, Barbados, Paradise Island, St. Thomas, St. Maarten, Jamaica, Cabo San Lucas, and Grand

Bahama were just a few of the favorite destinations I enjoyed using my timeshare. The weather was always perfect that time of year. I was surrounded by the beautiful aquamarine ocean, every destination was very welcoming to tourists, and each country lived by the mantras "Enjoy life," "Don't worry, be happy," and "No problem, Mon."

My Annual ME-TREAT Schedule

For the first few years of my ME-TREATS, the schedule went something like this: I would spend the first three days sleeping in, vegging on the couch, watching movies, taking island tours, shopping, enjoying the sunrise and sunset on the beach, eating all of the lobsters my heart desired (yes, I'm a seafood lover), and enjoying the peace and serenity and the sounds of the ocean. It would usually take me three to four days just to decompress and shift my mind from the hustle and bustle of everyday work and home responsibilities to vacation mode.

On the third or fourth day (when my mind was clear), I'd pull out my laptop and open my document called "New Year's Resolutions/Goals." I would review what I had written on the previous ME-TREAT. Throughout the year I would have pulled them out to update my progress, but life and work were so fast paced and hectic and I had so many things going on that I didn't have much time to review them. Getting away for vacation each year was my time to assess how effective I had been at accomplishing those resolutions.

While reviewing my goals, I'd write down all of the accomplishments from that year that I should be proud of. Then I'd reflect on what goals were not completed and why, and determine if they should be transferred to the new year or abandoned altogether. I would also document some of the lessons I had learned that year. Going through this exercise was cathartic and made me feel proud and at peace. It was not that everything had gone perfect in my life that year, nor had I accomplished all that I had planned for the year, but I was honest with myself and committed to working on me and to doing better each year.

So often we go through life without slowing down to take inventory of where we are, to count our blessings, smell the flowers, and celebrate our milestones. Not that we have to do this every day or every week, but it should be something we do often. When we don't do this, we allow so much time to pass and we forget about the things we've accomplished and all that has happened in our life. Doing this review helps us to offset some of the challenges we face, including some of the bad things that can overshadow our dreams and aspirations.

After reviewing my resolutions and identifying what I had accomplished (and had not accomplished), I'd begin the process of setting new resolutions and goals. When that ritual was completed I'd do something to celebrate. I would start with toasting myself with a chilled bottle of my favorite sparkling cider; then I'd make dinner reservations at one of the local restaurants that came highly recommended by the hotel's concierge. I'd ask for a special table, indicating that I was celebrating a special occasion. I'd put on a nice outfit and enjoy a full-course meal and all of the special treatment from the restaurant staff.

On the last two days of my ME-TREAT I'd take it easy and soak up the sun while sitting on the beach and listening to the sounds of the waves. I could hear myself thinking clearer and dreaming bigger dreams by the water. Oh, how I dreamed of living this life one day. I'd pull out my journal and, like I did as a kid, allow my imagination to run wild and take me on an adventure down Possibility Parkway.

The Return of My Dreams and Imagination

After all of the devastating experiences that had derailed my dreams and taken away my personal power, I started to imagine all of the things I could see myself doing beyond my present circumstances—wishing and hoping that one day they would come true. My new list of dreams included the following:

- Opening up a success center—a studio where I could do coaching and conduct workshops and seminars on communication, professional etiquette, and public speaking
- Running a state scholarship pageant system for young girls
- Winning a title as a national pageant queen

- Being promoted and making a six-figure salary and having no financial worries
- Launching my own consulting and training firm
- Meeting the man of my dreams (again) and enjoying a healthy and fulfilling relationship
- Living in a resort-style community, near the beach, that would feel like I was on vacation year-round
- Traveling, speaking, and being known all over the world for delivering a transformational message and for being an expert on certain knowledge
- Hosting my own talk show
- Writing lots of books that would be on shelves in major bookstores around the world

Yes, these were lofty dreams, and I wrote them all down in my journal. Interestingly enough, they didn't change much from year to year. I kept imagining the same dreams every year, which to me indicated that I must be destined to achieve them. Unfortunately, for the first few years of my ME-TREATS I'd go back home, unpack my suitcases, put the journal with all of those dreams in the top drawer of my nightstand, and print out my New Year's resolutions and goals, which I'd place on top of my journal, with the intention to review them every month. Notice I said *intention*.

Repeating a Cycle

Within a few days I was back to my routines of work, home, and mommy duties, and before I knew it weeks and months had passed before I reviewed my goals. When I did, I hate to admit it, still slipped into the abyss of doubt and fears by asking myself, What if I try opening the success center and go broke? What if I start dating now as a single mom and get my heart broken again? What if I don't pass that certification course? What if I write that book and it doesn't sell? My answers would be based on all of the limits and obstacles in my way at the time, so I would talk myself out of taking the risk. I would go back to life as usual.

Even though I was on this journey of self-care, self-reflection, and self-discovery, I was still repeating a cycle. It was frustrating to be both stuck and in a comfort zone at the same time while trying to break out. I had made so much progress on my journey, but I was still getting in *my* way. I was still allowing my past to disrupt, derail, and delay my future by what I thought and what I spoke to myself.

My Personal Change Management Process

Over the years I've come to the recognize that what I was experiencing was my own personal change management process. Interestingly enough, this process would become part of my life's work, but I didn't know it at the time. It was many years later that I realized that I had to go through the process first so that I could be more effective in helping others go through the same process. This realization ultimately helped me to be more effective in my HR and consulting work because I understood how difficult change can be. It's uncomfortable, it's risky and it's unknown, and none of us like that kind of uncertainty. We like to hold on to the familiar and to what we think we can control. But change is a process of letting go of the old and embracing the new.

One of the resources that helped me get through my change process was a book on change management by William Bridges called *Transitions*.[1] It was recommended to me by a mentor when I was going through some job changes, but oh did it help me as well with some personal changes I was experiencing.

Bridges identifies three stages of transition that people go through. Stage 1 is called Endings. In this stage we experience anxiety, sadness, frustration, and loneliness, and even depression might occur.

In stage 2, the Neutral Zone, we tend to be impatient, confused, or insecure as we are getting used to new processes, procedures, and relationships and to a new reality. Even though the worst part of the change we experienced in stage 1 may be past us, we still struggle with various lingering feelings such as anxiety, resentment, and anger.

This is where I was stuck—in the Neutral Zone, the in-between time. As I tried to move beyond my past and embrace a new mindset, I felt anxious, scared, and insecure. I had done some in-depth work on myself by addressing my disempowering beliefs and present bias, by confronting my fears, and by letting go of other self-sabotaging behaviors, but I hadn't quite arrived yet at what Bridges describes as stage 3, the New Beginnings stage.

During this phase, he says, we experience new energy and come to accept the change we are undergoing. We may see the first results and benefits of that change and find it to be acceptable or better than expected, and thus be willing to invest in and commit to it. Our attitude and our actions may change to align with our new beginning. It would be a few more months before I started seeing tangible benefits, but I was determined to move forward and not stay stuck in neutral.

That year I took more aggressive actions to break the cycle I kept repeating. I knew I wanted more out of life and I was feeling some anxiety about getting older and not having accomplished many of my dreams. I was in search of significance and purpose and I wasn't fulfilled. I made a commitment to invest more in my development and to build more confidence by reading more books, listening to motivational messages, getting a mentor, and attending seminars and workshops. That year I attended Oprah's Live Your Best Life Tour and it lit a fire under me. I read the *New York Times* best-selling book by Rick Warren called *The Purpose Driven Life* and it taught me to be specific and deliberate in writing down my purpose statement. I then had the pleasure of meeting world-renowned motivational speaker Les Brown while attending a conference, and we became fast friends. He immediately pointed out gifts and talents that I had shelved for years, and some I hadn't seen in myself. He invited me to attend a speaking seminar he was hosting later that year called Live Your Dreams, and I agreed to make the investment.

It turned out to be one of the best decisions and most transformational relationships of my life. That event enabled me to further strengthen my purpose statement and establish my life plan, and I secured an opportunity to be personally mentored and coached by Les. I earned the designation of being one of his Platinum Speakers, which afforded me the opportunity to travel with him for five years, speaking on stages and at organizations around the world. That year was my breakthrough and breakout moment, and my life took a dramatic turn for the better. By traveling with Les Brown and observing and attending these events as a speaker, coach, and entrepreneur, I saw what success really looked like. I internalized the feedback and coaching he gave me and was finally experiencing the benefits of change that Bridges referred to as stage 3: New Beginnings.

That year's ME-TREAT was like none before it. I was fired up and armed with more information, resources, and motivation than I'd had in prior years. I still followed a schedule similar to what I had followed in the past, but this year on the fourth day, when it came time to set new goals and resolutions, I instead pulled out my purpose statement and the life plan I had drafted. I had never before had these items written down so succinctly and so aligned with my purpose. They had become so much clearer as I read Rick Warren's book and many others, listened to the words that Les Brown spoke into my life, and followed the advice of others I trusted.

Moving Beyond New Year's Resolutions to a Purpose and a Life Plan

This year's ME-TREAT was a game changer in helping me begin to realize my dreams. For the first five years of these ME-TREATS I set New Year's resolutions and made empty promises to myself. For example, I set a resolution to work out every day at the gym, eat healthier, and lose ten to fifteen pounds by April; to save thousands of dollars by the end of the year; to get out of debt; and to learn a second language. Turns out that these are the most common resolutions that people set year after year.

According to *U.S. News and World Report*, more than 40 percent of us make resolutions, and at the end of the year only 8 percent of us feel we were successful in achieving our goals. In fact, on average, 80 percent of resolutions fail by the second week of February each year.[2] I was among those resolution breakers. I can't remember ever going to the gym every day, so the money spent on a gym membership every January was a total waste. I never learned a second language fluently, nor did I lose ten pounds by April, or by July, or by November. In fact, I gained a few extra pounds. You get the point.

Understanding Your Purpose

Understanding your purpose starts with the most basic questions in life: Who am I? Why am I here? When you start answering these questions you'll bring new meaning to every aspect of your life—to your career, to your relationships, and to your responses to life's challenges. Too many people live their life frustrated because they have no idea what they want to become or why they were created. They spend years in search of significance, like I did, trying to find their *why,* yet so few live a fulfilling and meaningful life.

For many years I've said that many people die at age thirty but don't get buried until age 85. Why? Because they don't have meaning, significance, or a clear vision for their life. They go through life wandering, seeking direction, dreaming and imagining but never implementing, and by the time they are older they've got more regrets than achievements. It's been said that the poorest person in the world is the one without a dream or vision, and the most frustrated person in the world is the one with a dream or vision who places it on pause and never achieves it.

In order to find significance, we must have a purpose and a life plan. Purpose is what you were created and born to do. It's your *why.* It's the reason you're wired the way you are. It's the reason you possess the kinds of skills and talents you have. Purpose has to do with your destiny (or your destination). It drives you and makes you get out of bed every morning. It gives you a strong sense of self-worth and a dose of energy and passion for life. And it guides your choices and decisions. I believe you have no limitations except the ones you have accepted from others and those that you have imposed on yourself. If you truly know why you were born and how gifted and talented and valuable you are, then you have to believe there's nothing you can't achieve.

My purpose statement is *to train, coach, teach, and empower others with knowledge, strategies, and skills, and to enable them to see a larger vision for themselves so that they find meaning, fulfillment, and success in every area of their life.* Yes, this was my goal in life even while I had not yet attained these things for myself. But I came to understand that all of my experiences, good and bad, all of the lessons I was learning and the journey I was on were preparing me for this assignment that was imminent in my future. Do you know your purpose? Have you written it down? How are your life experiences preparing you for what you are destined to achieve?

Once you know your purpose you can draft your own life plan. That year I had developed one for the first time in my life, and I aligned it with all of the dreams I had written down year after year—the dreams that got placed in my nightstand and collected dust, never getting fulfilled. Since that time more than twenty years ago, I have never been without a life plan. I refresh it often as my life and needs change. I pray over it, I track it, and I celebrate milestones along the way. It is my road map and my GPS for my life.

How to Develop Your Life Plan

A life plan is a written outline of the visions, dreams, and goals you want to accomplish within a certain time frame. It documents your purpose and priorities and provides a clear path for decision-making. It also brings your thoughts to life and manifests your dreams. I developed five categories of goals for my life plan: (1) career/professional, (2) health/wellness, (3) personal relationships/home life, (4) finances, and (5) spirituality. For example, my career goals have included working toward a higher position, completing a certification, or applying for a promotion; and my financial goals might include saving a certain amount of money, paying off a bill, or giving more money to charities.

A major consideration in creating a life plan is to remain flexible and make it a living, breathing document that is updated according to how your life changes and as you evolve and mature. Just like a phone app that can prompt you to do things, or like a GPS that gives you directions, so does a life plan. It is important to write down your plan, because a written plan is easier to remember, helps you to stay focused, and frees your mind to focus on other things. We have hundreds of thoughts every minute, and we cannot remember everything we think. some of my best ideas have flowed when I've been in the shower or driving my car, but later I forget many of those great ideas. Has this ever happened to you? I have learned to write down my great ideas as soon as I can and to keep my phone nearby so I can jot them down or quickly voice record them on one of my apps. This is also how I keep my life plan updated and refreshed.

Another key consideration I have found for developing a life plan is to take a self-assessment of where you are. This assessment requires you to be open, authentic, and honest with yourself. You have to be willing to call out your areas that need improvement, your fatal flaws, and your failures. I know it's easy to list your strengths and focus on them, but when you don't grow and develop new skill sets, mindsets, attitudes, and behaviors, you can become obsolete and complacent.

It is also important to identify the core values you live by. Why? Because when you are faced with decisions, you can measure your options against your values and choose the option that best aligns with your priorities or that moves you forward toward realizing your dreams. Whether it's a simple decision, such as whether to spend money on something you don't really need or save your money to fulfill a dream of starting your own business, or a major decision, such as a career change, a life plan helps you decide clearly what is right for you. Sticking to your core values can also help you deprioritize things that take up a lot of your time but have no relationship to your purpose. In other words, it will give you a reason to say no. Examples of core values include integrity, honesty, respect, family, loyalty, commitment, authenticity, and spirituality.

Another step in creating your life plan is to think long-term, mid-term, and short-term. Identify where you see yourself in ten years, five years, and three years. Then list your overall goal for what you want to achieve in one year and the most important tasks that will get you there. Break up those tasks by quarter, then by month, then by week.

The last thing I included in my life plan was specific milestones and what success would look like. That way I had a means to measure my progress along the way.

Developing and living by my life plan gave me a whole new ritual that set my life on a very different path. As I mentioned, for the first five years of my ME-TREATS I focused on setting a bunch of nice resolutions that sounded good but were actually empty promises that I didn't follow through on with serious commitment. But for the next five years I focused on implementing my life plan and achieving my dreams.

The year in which I created my life plan I had been aggressive and invested in my development like never before. It was a defining time in my life. I confronted my own insecurities, shortcomings, and limitations that kept me from discovering my purpose and establishing a life plan. I challenged beliefs about myself that kept me asking, "What if?" I became a producer instead of a procrastinator. I conquered my fears and learned how to take risks in pursuit of my dreams. It wasn't easy, but it was necessary. I also wasn't finished. I was a work in progress. I had just begun, and it was the start of a life-changing and lifelong journey toward realizing my dreams. For the next five years of ME-TREATS, I saw my life continue on a positive path and began to see many of my dreams come to pass. I was no longer searching for significance; I had found it. Now I was producing evidence of success and was no longer hindered by disempowering beliefs or self-sabotaging actions.

Chapter 6

RELATIONSHIPS ARE THE NEW CURRENCY

*G*ood relationships are the foundation for success in all areas of life. We are social creatures. In fact, one of the most basic needs we have as human beings is the need for connection and belonging. We need it just as much as we need food, water, and security. Relationships are essential to meeting this basic need no matter our age, our nationality, or our gender. Without relationships, life can be useless, boring, and lonely. Being in healthy relationships can provide you with life energy that nurtures you from within. And it can bring you greater fulfillment, open new doors, and expand your knowledge and perspective.

Practicing Self-Love

My religious faith taught me at an early age that one of the Ten Commandments required me to love my neighbors as I love myself. Through my faith, parental teaching, and life experiences, I have come to believe that the most important relationship in life is with yourself. If you don't love yourself entirely, take care of yourself consistently, and ensure that your own needs are met and that you are at your best, you will find it difficult to do the same for other people.

The way you treat yourself determines how you will treat others. I've come to believe that practicing self-care isn't being selfish, and being self-centered is necessary self-care. I don't mean that in the negative sense, that no one else matters. Rather, once you become grounded and centered in your own well-being (mind, body, and spirit), serving and empowering others will come naturally.

To feel your best, do your best work, and achieve your dreams, you have to be centered on building your self-esteem, sense of self-worth, and self-confidence. Much of this book has been about doing the work within. It's been about releasing the limits you have placed on yourself and getting out of your own way so you can realize your dreams. This is self-love at its best.

It is impossible to dream and imagine your life being better in the future if you aren't mentally, emotionally, and physically ready to respond. Some opportunities come only once, others may come occasionally, and sometimes they come often; but whenever they come, you don't want to miss out simply because you haven't done the internal work. Some of the best advice I have received is that it's better to be prepared for an opportunity and never have one than to have an opportunity present itself and not be prepared. That's the worst feeling you can have. In this book, you've read my stories about not being ready and what it cost me. I hope you've learned how important it is to stay on the journey of self-love and self-development and to build a great relationship with yourself, because it is the key to your success.

How Do You Know You Love Yourself?

For years a question I asked myself was, How do you really know you love yourself? Having been through the process of self-development and overcoming self-defeating beliefs, I offer here a few ways to know if you are in a great relationship with yourself. Some of these statements were shared by many of my mentors and advisers who experienced similar journeys toward self-love. Review the list and rate yourself on which of these statements are true about you and which you need to work on.

1. You are true to yourself (meaning you are honest with yourself about where you are in life and about your strengths, shortcomings, needs, hurts, feelings, and so on).

2. You accept your flaws and your mistakes, and you don't dwell on them.

3. You are kind to others.

4. You don't seek validation from external sources, such as social media.

5. You value your alone time.

6. You celebrate yourself.

7. You take care of your mental and physical health.

8. You manage your finances responsibly.

9. You have a positive attitude.

10. You are grateful for what you have.

Building Relationships with Others

Personal Board of Advisers

Once you establish the most important relationship in life, it is critical to surround yourself with two other groups of people. The first group is what I call my personal board of advisers—my closest and most trusted family members, friends, and colleagues. If you have them, you could also include your spouse, partner, spiritual leader, and others. My board of advisers has built me up, pushed me forward, made me better, and provided the kind of support that has enabled me to realize my dreams. They know how I think and what my strengths and weaknesses are, so they know how to support me personally and professionally.

Through the years, they have been instrumental in my growth, my recovery from failures, and my reinvention. I am so grateful to call my mom, dad, brothers, and daughter my biggest cheerleaders, confidants, and members of my personal board of advisers. Additionally, my best friend of more than thirty years and a few of my colleagues and clients who have become close friends are also part of that elite and small circle of advisers.

Building an Extended, Diverse Network

Second, I have an extended network that provides me great counsel and wisdom from their experience, and they share resources that help me in my career and business endeavors. It has been said that it's not what you know, it's who you know, and this couldn't be a truer reason for having a network. I consider myself a master connector and an effective relationship builder, and I have experienced the value that having a great network can bring.

A professional network consists of a group of individuals with whom you connect and build relationships that will enable you to advance your goals and access new opportunities and resources. Unfortunately, I have found that not everyone knows how to build an effective, diverse network, so here are some strategies I used to build mine.

First, assess your current network. I know it's human nature to want to be around people who are just like you. However, I cannot overstate how important it is in a multicultural, multigenerational, and globally diverse world to surround yourself with people who will help you expand your thinking and grow your ability to work, live, and lead effectively and succeed in this new demographic reality. Likewise, having a lot of people around you is not as beneficial as having the right people in your network. It's about quality over quantity. That means having a professional network of people from all walks of life who are different from you—various ethnicities, genders, cultures, ages, beliefs, personalities, experiences, skill sets, thinking styles, and the like. I began building this kind of network early in my career. Such a broad network makes for a rich and beautiful tapestry of unique gifts and talents that can contribute great value to you.

Ask yourself these key questions:

a. Who are the people currently in my network?

b. Why did I select them, or vice versa?

c. What skills, experience, and resources do they offer?

d. Does everyone in my network look, think, and act like me?

Once you have answered these questions, you will have a better idea of who you already have and who else you need to invite into your network. For me, this approach really yielded tangible benefits. For example, when I relocated to another state a few years ago, I didn't know anyone in the area. I accessed LinkedIn and joined a few professional groups in my region; I also sent invitations to connect to HR professionals and diversity and inclusion practitioners in my area. Another example was when I was working on a large culture transformation project for a client and they wanted to know how other companies had approached the same work and what some best practices and trends were. I sent out a message to a number of people in my network who I knew had experience and success. I was able to get from them a lot of great resources, lessons, and tips that enabled me to achieve better results for that client, and it saved me so much time. More recently, I was seeking a candidate with specific skills in auditing and research. The first thing I did was reach out to my network to solicit recommendations. I received a number of responses and within a few days I was scheduling interviews with several qualified candidates, and ultimately hired one.

Second, while attending live social events such as conferences, conventions, seminars, or workshops, look for opportunities to initiate a conversation. I do this often and here's the approach I take. Let's say you're at the conference reception or at a table for lunch or sitting beside someone in a session. Take the first step and initiate a conversation. Get to know who they are, what they do, and about their experiences and expertise. I usually start the conversation with "Hi, I'm Dr. Shirley Davis, CEO of SDS Global Enterprises." They usually return the same information about themselves. Then I'll ask something like, "Have you attended this conference before?" or "What made you attend this seminar?" Take it from there and see where it goes.

Look for commonalities; perhaps you work in the same industry, are at the same level in your career, are from the same geographic location, have the same kind of business, and so on. Use that information to further the conversation. Should you find them interesting and possessing diverse skills you can benefit from, ask them if they would be open to connecting with you on your social media platform, such as LinkedIn, Twitter, Instagram, Facebook, and the like.

This leads me to the third way to build an extended, diverse network: connect online. I conduct searches on those same social media sites, and I conduct other Internet searches to find professionals who share my interests and have unique skills and expertise that I can benefit from, and I invite them to connect. Also, when I come across someone's online post that interests me, I engage with them by responding and thanking them for their posts. Then I send them an invitation to connect, stating that I like to learn from interesting people like them and add them to my network. What I learned in implementing these three steps is that identifying the right people is about being intentional and strategic in who you invite and why.

Benefits of a Broad, Diverse Network: *Leveraging My Network for Career Success*

As a woman, a minority, and a young professional, I didn't see many people who looked like me at the top of many organizations and I knew I would need the support of others to get there. I built relationships and a broad network of professionals who taught me how to navigate inside an organization as a minority, a woman, a single mom, and other underrepresented traits; how to position myself as a leader; and how to communicate my value.

I also leveraged my relationships to increase my knowledge and skills, to learn more about the industries I worked in, and to get access to resources. As a result, I worked my way up to senior leadership and executive roles and enjoyed tremendous success later in my career. And now, as the owner of a global workforce solutions firm, having those broad relationships has been critical to my success and to the many opportunities that have come my way via referrals and recommendations. Several of my contacts were converted to contracts.

I'm a big believer that people come across your path for a reason and you must nurture each relationship in such a way that it yields benefits to both people. Here are two examples of relationships I nurtured.

A Partnership with Grace

For more than ten years I enjoyed a mutually beneficial relationship with a colleague I met at work named Grace. She was a well-respected consultant and speaker and was passionate about her work in leadership, change management, and diversity. When we first met in 2005, we became fast friends as well as professional colleagues. We spoke at conferences together, served on committees, referred business to each other, and collaborated on books, white papers, and training programs. One year she landed a multiyear contract with a large bank in the northeast part of the United States. She was ecstatic and they loved her work.

A few years into the contract, she suffered a stroke and lost her ability to speak clearly and to walk or stand for long periods, among other things. This was a devastating event because it was unexpected and it took away one of her main sources of income and something she was gifted in—speaking and singing. She had a voice like an angel, and I remember her opening a conference I hosted with a beautiful rendition of "Amazing Grace."

After weeks of being in the hospital, she reached out to me and requested that I take on one of her major clients while she rehabilitated. She indicated that she trusted me with her business and with this client and knew they would receive me well. I agreed and immediately began delivering coaching and training to them with another colleague she had also reached out to. For the next year she continued to develop new training courses for the client and to work behind the scenes to support us in delivering.

One evening I reached out to her to get last-minute updates and to let her know I had arrived at the hotel safely and was all set for the next day of training. We spoke and she was thrilled to know that everything was good. But she wasn't feeling well that evening and let me know she had been in the hospital a few days that week.

The next day I reached out again and left her a message saying that the sessions were well received again and the client was satisfied. I didn't hear back from her, but I figured she was resting and recuperating. Two days later I received a message that she had passed away the day I left her that message. I was devastated! It was unbelievable news. Later that afternoon I called the client to ask if they knew of her passing, and they had not heard. They too were devastated. A week later, the client called me and wanted to talk about next steps with the contract. She said, "Because *she* trusted you with us, *we* trust you with us," and the contract was transferred to me for another year.

While this story is quite sad, it really is a story about the power of relationship. Over the years we had nurtured a trusting, respectful, and mutually beneficial relationship that turned into a business opportunity for both of us. I was able to step in and partner with her in her darkest hour and in her last days, and she trusted me enough to serve her client. As a result, her client trusted me because *she* trusted me. This is what I mean when I say that relationships are the new currency.

An Encounter with Les Brown

One year I attended a conference while enjoying a vacation cruise with my mom. We had just left a session and were heading back to our cabin. We were standing in front of the elevator door waiting for it to return to the lower level, where we were. Finally it arrived, and when the elevator door opened I saw a crowd of people packed in like sardines. As another crowd of us awaited their exit, I looked up and saw Les Brown in the center of the crowd inside the elevator. Yes, *the* Les Brown, world-renowned motivational speaker, best-selling author, radio personality, and "Mrs. Mamie Brown's Baby Boy."

We locked eyes and he immediately walked over to me with two others (who turned out to be his daughter and one of his assistants). He looked at me and said, "You look familiar, do I know you?" I knew who he was because I had been listening to his motivational speeches for years. A year earlier I had spoken at a conference where he was the headliner and had participated on a panel in my role as Ms. American United States Woman, but we hadn't gotten to meet in person because I had to leave immediately following my session. That's the only time we were in the same room, so I shared that incident with him and assumed that must have been why I looked familiar.

Turns out that's where he remembered me from. He didn't remember my name, but he remembered me participating as Ms. American United States Woman. I went on to mention that I had listened to several of his motivational speeches, including "Live Your Dreams" and "It's Not Over Until You Win," and I commented on how much they had inspired me during my pursuit of the crown. I told him I had just completed my reign and had crowned my successor a few months earlier and was treating mom to some rest and relaxation on vacation.

Naturally we connected, because we were fellow speakers, but from that day forward we were fast friends. He invited me to attend his sessions on the cruise and insisted that mom and I have dinner at his table. When the ship stopped at various islands, he invited mom and I to tag along with a few others, including his daughter and some other friends. I had no idea where this was going but I pinched myself a few times because I couldn't believe what was happening.

Mom and I had the best time and enjoyed getting to know Les. He was down-to-earth, had the most infectious laugh, and told so many stories and jokes, and nobody was a stranger. He would walk down the halls and on the decks of the ship and just stop and talk to people like he had stopped and talked to me. But I was invited to be a part of his entourage. It would be a game-changing experience for me and I knew that purpose had collided with opportunity.

As the cruise came to an end six days later, Les invited me to attend one of his upcoming speaker training workshops. I agreed to do so, and the rest is destiny (not history, but part of a divine plan). After attending his speaker training workshop I was never the same. I learned so much and even won one of his speech competitions. Sound familiar? Yes, I won my first speech competition in my first pageant at the age of thirteen, and now I had come full circle to be exposed to someone like Les Brown.

Under his tutelage I found my voice and my purpose, developed my life plan, and gained a mentor and ultimately a good friend. I sharpened my public speaking skills and won a spot as one of his Platinum Speakers. For five years I had the honor of traveling with Les and a few of his other Platinum Speakers all over the world, and it gave me the courage, the hunger, and the determination to push myself even more toward achieving my dreams. He was there rooting me on and encouraging me to jump and grow my wings on the way down. (I share more about this idea in the next chapter.) He provided me with resources and was constantly pitching me to conference and meeting planners. He urged me to write my first two books and has become one of my biggest brand ambassadors.

He also wrote the foreword for this book, and throughout my writing it he would check in on my progress. When I finished writing it, he helped market it by hosting me on his daily Facebook Live show, mentioning it in other forums where he was speaking, and encouraging all of his followers to purchase the book. He bragged about me and this book like a proud papa. I am forever grateful for these kinds of relationships, because they have made me a better person. From Les Brown to my best friend of more than thirty years, Dr. Luquanda Neekey Hawkins, to my parents, my daughter, my spiritual leaders, and a few trusted advisers, many have contributed to the success I enjoy today. They have helped me get out of my own way, move beyond my "What if?" questions, and live over here on this side of my dreams.

Other Benefits of Having a Strong Network

Having a strong and diverse network of people has many other benefits and advantages. I am often asked how I am able to get so much done and achieve so many things. My response is always that I have an awesome network of strong relationships that I access, and they help me to save time, money, and unnecessary effort. Additionally, there are a myriad of other benefits and advantages to having diverse and strong relationships. Here are six more that I have enjoyed; that have been instrumental in my ability to overcome personal, organizational, and societal barriers and limitations; and that have contributed to my ability to realize my dreams.

First, when I started my career in human resources, I joined several organizations, read a lot of books, and subscribed to a number of online platforms. But it wasn't until I made the human connections with professionals who possessed diverse expertise, skills, and backgrounds in HR that I began to grow new skills. They shared best practices and pitfalls, and offered resources and learning opportunities that gave me an edge and cut my learning curve in half.

Second, by leveraging my relationships I obtained new job opportunities. When the time came for me to move into new roles, I reached out to my network to inquire about what was available. Many of them referred me to their companies or to other jobs they were aware of and offered to be references. They also recommended me to recruiters and to job sites that expanded my search. As a result, I was often able to secure a new opportunity.

Third, meeting new people has been a great advantage to having a broad network. I meet many of them on social media, through community groups, online events, and virtual introductions. And as I travel all over the world and speak at conferences and companies of all types, I am intentional about meeting new people, fostering relationships, and inviting people to be a part of my network. This approach allows me to expand my knowledge and my exposure to different cultures, countries, and backgrounds.

Fourth, receiving feedback and coaching has been one of the most significant benefits of having a broad array of relationships. I have learned so many perspectives, ideas, and solutions from people with varying experiences and backgrounds that I wouldn't have learned otherwise. I have become a better person personally and professionally because I not only solicit feedback but also welcome unsolicited coaching. Feedback and coaching have contributed to my journey of overcoming the many obstacles I faced that limited my thinking and believing.

Fifth, I can't tell you how much obtaining new referrals and recommendations has accelerated my career and my business success. As I mentioned earlier, when I needed to learn about my industry, to understand trends and best practices, and to obtain resources that would help me complete a project or prepare for a new assignment, my network was a great source. Also, I led recruiting for more than ten years and I can tell you that even today recruiting firms reach out to me requesting referrals and asking me who I know who can fill the roles they are seeking to fill. Many people I know got their jobs through referrals from someone they knew. New job opportunities are all about relationships. As president of my consulting firm, I am pleased to tout that more than 95 percent of my business is driven by referrals, repeat business, live events, and my presence on social media—building connections and new relationships. Of course this success requires that I deliver value, but it also requires that I give more than is expected. When this happens, clients and colleagues are more than happy to refer me to others.

Sixth, having a broad array of relationships has enhanced my health and well-being. We are all social beings and need connection. So, when I needed encouragement, support, and advice when faced with my many fears, excuses to put my dreams on hold, disempowering "What if?" questions, and the temptation to give up, it was my network that helped me get through these tough transitions and challenging times.

Today I have mastered the art of building and fostering great relationships in both my business and my personal life, and they have added tremendous value to my heart, my soul, my well-being, and my business success. Over the years I have learned that people hire, promote, pay more, and do business with people they *know*, *like*, and *trust*. I often say that it's not just what you know or who you know but what they know about you. Having a loving relationship with yourself and learning the art of building beneficial relationships, as well as knowing how to leverage those relationships in a way that helps you learn, grow, and become better, are critical ingredients in achieving your dreams.

Last but most important, while I consider myself a master connector and an effective relationship builder, I would be remiss if I didn't recognize the most important relationship in my life—my vertical spiritual relationship with my Creator. It is this relationship that is the foundation to who I am, what I am becoming, what I believe, and how I live my life.

It is on this relationship that I have relied the most to guide, protect, and sustain me through the toughest and most difficult times and that has brought me the most calm and peace when everything around me has seemed to be falling apart. And it is this relationship that I believe has ultimately directed my steps to the right people, whom I have surrounded myself with and who have contributed to my success and helped me get to this state of living beyond "What if?"

Chapter 7

JUMP AND GROW YOUR WINGS ON THE WAY DOWN

s I just shared in the previous chapter, my mentor and coach Les Brown used to say to me, "Shirley, jump and grow your wings on the way down." I didn't understand what he meant at first, but he clarified after saying it to me many times. He explained that there comes a time when we've done all we can do to prepare, a time when we cannot remain in our comfort zone, when we should not continue to dodge the things that cause us to fear. He would say, "Shirley, you're prepared—you have multiple certifications; you've taken all of the courses; you have a master's degree, a Ph.D.; you've attended numerous conferences. I've been your coach for years; you've got the knowledge; you're a phenomenal speaker; you've got what it takes to succeed—now it's time for you to jump. You will figure it out."

For years that advice haunted me, motivated me, and paralyzed me all at the same time. But it ultimately resonated with me. What I came to realize from that one statement was that I shouldn't keep waiting and waiting for my wings to grow and expand before I leapt. I couldn't keep waiting for things to be perfect. I couldn't wait for all of the answers to be in place. And I couldn't stay stuck on all of my "What if?" questions. I had to go do something; I had to take a risk if I was going to realize my dreams. And I had to make up my mind to jump.

Most People Are Afraid of Jumping

Most people are afraid to step outside their comfort zone to pursue their dreams, because they are afraid that something may go wrong, that all of their fears and "What if?" questions may come true. As I have shared in previous chapters, one of the greatest barriers to achieving our dreams is fear. That's why we resist change, because it represents the unfamiliar, unknown, and uncomfortable. It was why I resisted pursuing many of the dreams I imagined for years. I had a lot of fears—fear of failing, fear of being broke, fear of rejection, fear of getting hurt, fear of the unknown, and fear that I couldn't maintain success if I achieved it.

Additionally, I had to overcome my reasons for procrastinating, to avoid being stuck in present bias, to dismantle my disempowering "What if?" questions and replace them with empowering responses, to discover my purpose, and to formulate my life plan. By taking this journey, I adopted a new way of thinking and believing, a new way of declaring victory, and most important, I built the courage, confidence, and discipline to finally take risks and pursue my dreams.

Muhammad Ali was considered one of the greatest heavyweight boxing champions of all time and was known for his courage, confidence, and discipline. He faced a number of challenges throughout his career, and even when he was considered the underdog and expected to lose a fight, he talked so confidently about beating his opponent that he won many of his fights in the mind first, meaning he convinced himself and the public that he *could* win long before the actual fight.

He would openly declare that he was "the greatest" and that he could "float like a butterfly and sting like a bee." And it didn't matter who he was fighting—his discipline, confidence, and public declarations never wavered. One of his most famous quotes was, "He who is not courageous enough to take risks will accomplish nothing in life."[1] I learned to do the same thing. There came a time when, as I was faced with challenges—no matter how big or small—I would face them head on by talking to myself out loud, declaring that I could do it, and then taking the risks.

Taking Calculated Risks

When I refer to taking risks I'm referring to calculated risks. Calculated risks are the actions we take after careful consideration of possible results and outcomes. It's been said that opportunities never look like opportunities. They come brilliantly disguised as problems and challenges. This means that in every situation we face, perspective is everything. It's how we look at a problem that can make the difference between being stuck or moving forward. I learned that it's not what happens to you, it's what you do with what happens to you. When these opportunities come our way, disguised as problems and challenges, we have to believe that they are happening for a greater purpose and that if we lean into them we can hopefully come out a stronger, wiser, and better version of ourselves.

When we do something or face something we've never experienced before, we should take calculated risks. We have to count the costs of our actions by predicting all that could go wrong or right and then ready ourselves to face it and take the leap. I'm not just talking about waking up one day and quitting your steady paying job simply because you have a dream to start a new business. You should conduct in-depth research about the market, determine the need for your product or service, conduct a competitive analysis, and determine pricing. This is the development of a business plan. By developing one, your chances of achieving success are much higher than those who launch without doing the due diligence.

Using My Courage to Jump toward a New Opportunity

I experienced what I call a game-changing event early in my career when I was working in HR. I was pretty comfortable working over in the "ivory tower" of human resources. At the time I had a great job as a senior HR consultant and was really enjoying some of the projects I had opportunity to work on. They were really visible projects in that they utilized a lot of my key skills and talents, and I was really passionate about the work I was doing. I had the autonomy, mastery, and purpose that best-selling author Daniel Pink outlined in his book *Drive*.

One day I got a call from a colleague in Operations asking if I would consider moving over to his division to head up training and development. But I was comfortable; I was enjoying what I was doing and, quite frankly, didn't think I needed to learn other skills. I enjoyed my nine-to-five schedule, rarely ever worked weekends, had the same clients I had built great relationships with, and had become quite comfortable serving. I can't tell you how much consternation I felt when my colleague asked me to step outside my comfort zone and step into an area that was completely unfamiliar territory. To be honest, it was having to work different shifts that included nights and weekends that wasn't appealing to me; plus, Operations spoke a whole different language, and the job meant a huge learning curve for me. Additionally, it meant having to make some major sacrifices at home because I was a single mom.

Despite my initial trepidation, I still gave it some thought, and I talked with a couple of my trusted colleagues and advisers about it. Eventually I agreed to jump and grow my wings on the way down. It was a risk to me because I was in uncharted territory and would have to build a whole new skill set, but it was a calculated risk that I was willing to take so that I could become more business savvy and expand my portfolio of experience. I jumped and it turned out to be one of the best career moves I made. The lessons in leadership, running a profit center, having a seat at the decision-making table in Operations, and learning the language of business all benefited me for the rest of my career.

When I built up the courage to jump and grow my wings on the way down, I asked challenging questions of myself and others. I learned that if we don't question our reality, in the long run we end up succumbing to it. Then later we realize that our silence has conditioned us and complied with our circumstances. Once I started jumping there was no turning back. Over a period of seven years I jumped and resigned from my job and launched my consulting firm, jumped and wrote my first book, jumped and left a bad relationship, and jumped and sold my home of fifteen years and relocated to another state. Here's how it happened.

I Jumped and Resigned
from My Job

It was in the eleventh year of my annual ME-TREAT that I finally felt the pull (or maybe it was the push) to pursue one of the big dreams that I had put off for years—launching my own consulting, speaking, and training firm. I had tried it on a small scale many times before but had starts and stops and failures. I never could get it off the ground because I was still battling with the limitations of procrastination, stuck in "present bias," and answering my disempowering "What if?" questions with the wrong responses. But after years of releasing the limits using the steps I laid out in previous chapters, I felt a liberation and a release. This ME-TREAT turned out to be pivotal. A peace, a calm, and an excitement came over me like never before. I had increased my confidence, faith, and courage to finally jump. And my first big jump was resigning from my job to launch my own business.

For more than thirty years I worked my way up the corporate ladder in Fortune 100 and Fortune 50 companies in nearly forty countries around the world and in various industries and sectors. At the time of this ME-TREAT I had been in my current role as vice president of Global Diversity, Inclusion, and Workforce Strategies for five years and I loved the work I was doing. It afforded me the opportunity to travel around the world, and I was thrilled to see the impact it was having on the profession and within my organization.

Under my leadership, the department had become known as a leading resource for workforce diversity and inclusion and had gained international recognition for providing cutting-edge strategies, development, and research for thousands of practitioners around the world. I had the pleasure of hosting an annual conference for more than a thousand industry HR and diversity and inclusion professionals; planning and producing a summit for more than one hundred global thought leaders, pioneers, and other business leaders; developing a number of education, training, and certification programs that yielded thousands of graduates and certificants; and initiating the development of the first ever national standards for practicing diversity and inclusion.

I was extremely proud of the results and successes I had achieved for the organization, but there was still something missing. There was a void in my heart that wasn't being filled. I wanted to do more, not just for my employer, not just in my role. I felt destiny calling me to something greater—something beyond the job and the employer. It was speaking, training, coaching, and consulting, but not just on human resources and diversity and inclusion. I wanted to help people walk through their personal reinvention journey.

I wanted to coach minorities like myself on how to overcome obstacles and barriers, and how to get a seat at the table. I wanted to work with young professionals on how to navigate their careers and build life skills that would enable their success early on. And I wanted to work specifically with women on how to build the confidence and skills to succeed in a male-dominated workforce. After all that I had been through, I felt a special calling to reach back and help others.

It was one of the hardest decisions I would have to make, because it was risky and scary. At that time in my career, I had obtained a senior executive role, reporting to the CEO and executive vice president, and had earned a seat at the table with chief executives and the board of directors. I had built up a great name brand and reputation in my profession, and I was earning a six-figure salary with executive benefits and perks. The scary part was letting go of a steady paycheck, health and dental insurance, a retirement plan into which the company contributed a percentage to its value, and the sense of job security. The risky part now was launching something I had no guarantees would succeed this time, and the reality that I could end up broke, unable to pay my bills, and not able to send my daughter off to college.

Thankfully I had done the work while on my journey of self-development. I had confronted my fears (outlined in chapter 4), but I knew that some new and some old fears might return and this dream would be put to the test. But it had been a dream of mine for a long time, so I knew it was part of my destiny, and I couldn't keep ignoring it.

Developing an Exit Strategy

Simply put, an exit strategy is a plan or road map for leaving your current situation and entering into your next chapter. It lays out the steps and strategies for how you will make the transition. It should also detail the financial implications, potential risks, and associated obstacles, as well as the expected outcomes and tangible benefits. In my work as an HR professional I had the opportunity to help develop exit strategies with several organizations. They used them all the time for mergers and acquisitions, for entering or exiting new markets, for discontinuing certain products or services, for releasing a strategic partnership with another business, and for selling or closing parts or all of a business. The strategies could range from three months to three years, depending on the complexity and size of the change.

When I wanted to move from one type of position to another in the same company, I created a well-thought-out exit strategy. For example, the first step I took was to research the types of jobs I thought would be a good fit for my skills, interests, and passions. Second, I would review past and current job openings in the company and find those that appealed to me. Then I would study the specific requirements, skills, and qualifications for the job and perform a gap analysis—what was required and what I currently possessed. Third, I would compare those requirements, skills and qualifications to my past and current job responsibilities, results, and performance feedback.

Fourth, I would have a conversation with my direct supervisor to discuss my interest and enlist his or her approval. When I received the supervisor's support, the fifth thing I would do is detail a plan for closing the skills and experience gap, including time frames, the training classes I would need to take, whom I could request to mentor me, and what projects would give me greater visibility and experience.

Sixth, I'd get to know some of the staff with those skill sets and knowledge of the department so I could learn more about the culture and the people. This step also afforded those staff an opportunity to get to know me so that if and when an opening became available I was well positioned to be considered a strong candidate.

This exit strategy resulted in two new job opportunities in one company and enabled me to work there five more years. I used similar strategies when I pursued new opportunities with other employers, except I would reach out to my contacts online who could provide insights about the company with which I was pursuing employment.

In another role, I worked with a senior leader to devise an exit strategy for her to move from leading a team to being an individual contributor. She had received a number of complaints about the way she treated her direct reports and several of them had left the company. But she was a top producer and ran a profitable division in the company, so none of the senior executives wanted her to leave. Rather than terminate her employment, they decided that she should be moved to a different role, one that didn't involve her leading a team.

I worked with her on identifying the appropriate role description in the appropriate division, and outlined a strategy for transitioning her team to another leader in a way that would save face. We specified timelines for her transition and implemented a communication plan. The exit strategy was executed with little disruption and ended up being a win-win for her, her team, and the organization.

The development and implementation of exit strategies is a natural part of life as we experience change and disruption. These strategies happen at work, in relationships, at home, and in other aspects of our personal lives. They may not be as formal as I have described, they may instead be informal and unwritten plans of action. For example, I developed an exit strategy when I needed to end a partnership/contract with a firm that was not providing me with the services that had been promised. When I knew the time had come to end a relationship that was not working for me, I thought about it for weeks and played out in my mind every scenario I thought would happen when I told him it was over. I even used an exit strategy when I felt it was time to find a new place of worship. I had been a member for a long time and was very involved in the ministries, but there came a time when I had outgrown it. I knew that my pastor would try to talk me out of leaving, and I rehearsed my response over and over.

There comes a time when you just know that you have to move on and pursue your next chapter. An exit strategy can assist you in mapping out the direction and plans to get from here to there. I have learned that in life not everything is meant to be forever; some things have an expiration date and we must discern when that time arrives.

After working in corporate America for nearly thirty years, my time arrived. I decided to finally take the leap of faith into launching my own business. The experience I had gained in my years of developing and implementing exit strategies at work helped me to gracefully make my own transition.

I Jumped and Left a Bad Relationship

When I developed my exit strategy to jump from my job and launch my own business, I knew I would have to address another area of my life that could determine my success or failure. I was in a relationship that I knew was going sour and not showing signs of improvement. The relationship was not helping me but rather hindering me and causing me a lot of anxiety, stress, and undue pressure. It was with someone who I knew could not handle my big dreams, because in my small successes he would minimize and criticize what I was doing. It got to a point where I wouldn't even share great news about or successes in my job, my community work, or other things, because I could see how it would deflate him.

He was dealing with his own issues of insecurity, self-doubt, procrastination, pride, and regrets, and he was constantly comparing his success to mine. In heated exchanges the bitterness would rear its ugly head in the form of name calling, complaining, and belittling me. Yet on the outside he projected a false sense of success and confidence and had convinced a lot of people that he was someone he wasn't. I had held out hope that things would change, but I finally realized that I was the one who had to change (my mind and my location).

Through a series of events and strategic moves, I cut off the relationship and lifted a huge weight from my life. That outcome alone was a big win toward accomplishing my dream, because with him I had begun to shrink, and I had delayed my dreams because of him..I didn't want to outshine him, because he was already insecure about the level of success I had achieved so far. In the previous chapter I laid out the importance of having the right relationships around you and that you have to love yourself first. Coming to that realization while creating my exit strategy helped me to jump out of that relationship, move forward, and have no regrets.

I Jumped and Launched My Global Consulting Firm

After leaving my job I took some time off to rest, reflect, and shift my mindset. It was definitely an adjustment to not get up every morning to check work emails or jump on an early morning call, to not drive across town and sit in hour-long traffic jams, and to not go into my office and greet my team. Eventually I adjusted and began working on the final details of my business launch (including designing my website, publishing my first book, setting up my home office, hiring a CPA, establishing the business name, and updating my social media sites).

I had saved enough money to finance my business for the first year if I needed it, but I had also joined a boutique consulting firm on a limited contract basis so that I could build my business while maintaining a steady revenue stream. I also reached out to my many well-wishers and made a formal announcement about my new company and reminded them I was open for business and available to serve them. This step resulted in several new contracts, and that's how I built my business—by leveraging my network, by referrals and repeat business, and from live events.

Over a period of eighteen months I built up enough business to require my full-time attention. I was able to end my contract with the boutique consulting firm and focus all of my time on serving my own clients (yes, I used an exit strategy for that too). I felt so empowered and proud of myself. I had not failed this time, after several other unsuccessful starts. I had learned that most businesses fail within the first three years, so I worked hard to avoid being that statistic again. I had not had to use my savings account, and I was on a steady trajectory of building a viable and profitable business. Jumping never felt so good and I had indeed grown my wings on the way down.

I Jumped and Wrote My First Book

After all that I had experienced over two decades, and after having done the work to overcome my own limitations I felt it was time to write a book and share the strategies and steps that had worked for me. I had been approached by a number of young women and other minorities, as well as by emerging professionals, to mentor and coach them. I did that for a number of years and all of them indicated how transformative my coaching was. I realized that I couldn't reach as many people as I wanted. A book or a radio show would be the best avenue to capture my tips and strategies and reach a broader audience.

For years I would set writing a book as a goal for the next year, but I kept procrastinating and making excuses that I was too busy or it was too expensive. Finally deciding to start my business gave me the push and incentive I needed. Every expert I had consulted urged me to write the book and use it as an introduction to my other services, such as seminars, workshops, and keynote speeches. In chapter 2 I shared how I finally overcame my procrastination and got the book written by recording it as an audiobook first and then transcribing it into written format.

Once I released the book, *Reinvent Yourself: Strategies for Achieving Success in Every Area of Your Life,"* I also released the other services in my business, and enjoyed tremendous success. The book was also translated into other languages and I was thrilled that companies were even purchasing it for their staff and inviting me to speak about the stories and strategies contained in the book. Turns out that many of them wanted their people to reinvent themselves so they could bring fresh ideas and creativity to the company, and have a better sense of personal well-being.

I had the pleasure of speaking at conferences and conventions all over the world and hearing from attendees how impactful and transformative the book was for them. Today I still receive testimonials about how the book has helped people to change their thinking, change their circumstances, and change their lives. This was exactly what I intended it to do, so once I jumped and published that book, within a year I jumped again and wrote a workbook to accompany *Reinvent Yourself.* It has been a profitable companion product in my business.

A few years later I jumped again to pen a book about my journey to obtain a seat at the table as a woman and person of color. In that book I shared the strategies I employed to take back my power and move up the career ladder to get those seats at the executive and boardroom tables. I titled that book *The Seat: How to Get Invited to the Table When You're Over-Performing and Undervalued.* It too has been all over the world and is having an impact on individuals and organizations. Had I not jumped and released those books, I'd still be coaching and mentoring a few people a year and missing opportunities to touch thousands of people all over the world.

I Jumped and Moved to a Place I Had Never Visited

I'm a big believer that when you put things out into the universe, destiny shows up. It is exactly how I found my new place to live. For years I had dreamed of living someplace tropical. I love the warm weather, and one of my favorite places in the world is by the water—not just any water, but clear aquamarine ocean water like the Caribbean Sea and the Gulf of Mexico, where I would get away for my annual ME-TREATS.

When I finally made the leap to leave corporate America and launch my own global consulting firm, I had been living in the District of Columbia (DC), Maryland, and Virginia area (affectionally called the DMV) for nearly thirty years. My home was in Maryland, I worked in Virginia, and I drove through DC to get to work and to serve many of my clients. The DMV was definitely a hustle-and-bustle filled with traffic jams, road construction, and impatient drivers. The DMV was also an expensive place to live, had brutal cold winters with lots of snow and ice, and offered a fast-paced lifestyle. I was ready for a change of pace and a better quality of life.

The fact that I had a consulting firm meant I could operate it from anywhere, so the sky was the limit, but I had some must-haves. First, I wanted to remain in the United States and on the East Coast. Second, I had to be near an international airport because I traveled nearly 80 percent of the time. Third, my new home had to have a warm climate year-round and be near clear blue water and beaches. Fourth, it had to have a lower cost of living than the DMV but be in a metropolitan area. And fifth, it had to have less traffic and congestion and a better quality of life than DC.

I have traveled to forty-eight states around the United States, but the state with the best beaches and all of my other must-haves was Florida. I was mostly interested in checking out Tampa Bay, Jacksonville, Clearwater, and St. Petersburg, which all were on the west coast of Florida, were cities with lower costs of living, and had less traffic. When I narrowed my options to these four cities, I posted on my social media pages that I was considering moving to Florida and was seeking ideas about which city to live in. A classmate from high school sent me a message indicating that she was a real estate agent in the Tampa Bay area and would be happy to host me for a tour of homes. I immediately accepted her invitation and made plans to meet up in Tampa. Interestingly enough, I had visited Florida many times but had never been to Tampa.

Over the next few weeks I did some research on the four cities I had narrowed my search to and decided that the best fit would be the Tampa, Clearwater, and St Petersburg area. I found that three of the cities were less than thirty miles apart from each other, which made my decision even easier. Most important, they all boasted of award-winning beaches year-round.

A month later I flew to Tampa and spent my birthday week exploring the culture and happenings in the three cities. Each day I would meet up with the real estate agent and she would take me from one community to the next. They all offered so many amenities and I was sold on the home prices, the close proximity of the airport and all of the cultural events, and how much there was to do in all three cities.

By the end of my visit I knew I wanted to live in the Tampa Bay area, but the real estate market was booming so much that finding a place that week was impossible. I instructed my agent to keep searching until something became available. Two months later she messaged me that one of the communities I loved had an available rental. Thanks to technology, that same day she videoconferenced me and gave me a tour of the home. It was perfect and I signed the lease agreement that day.

One month later I put my Maryland home up for sale and moved to Tampa. I was excited about my next chapter and had no regrets, nor was I inundated with disempowering "What if?" questions. My first weekend in Tampa I drove twenty-five minutes to one of the best beaches in the country, Clearwater Beach. I was in heaven and affirmed that I had finally realized my dream of living in paradise. I have now lived in Florida for five years and I still feel like I did the first time I visited Tampa Bay—at peace. Who would have thought that a place I had never visited before, a place I had only imagined, would be my heaven on earth? This was perhaps one of the boldest moves I made when I started jumping, but it is certainly one of the *best* jumps I've ever taken.

What Jumping and Taking Risks Taught Me

If we are ever to get beyond our "What if?" questions, release the limits, and realize our dreams, we have to take those first steps—make the decision to jump, calculate the cost, and devise a plan. The first time I jumped and took a risk (a calculated risk), I built three things—courage, confidence, and calculation. Courage drives confidence and belief in ourselves. It gives us the motivation and inspiration necessary to achieve our purpose in life. Courage forces us to think differently, be doubtful, and question what we already know. It makes us want to go further and have our own opinions about things. Developing courage takes time and patience, but we must never be afraid to take a risk and release our limitations.

I have learned that anything worth doing is worth planning to succeed, because if we don't, we are planning to fail. I have learned that life's most rewarding experiences come as a result of taking risks on yourself and your dreams and believing that those risks are worth taking. Even when we don't have guarantees, we have to rely on our determination, experience, and willingness to learn. I had jumped before and failed, but I learned what didn't work.

I can honestly admit that for more than a decade I had more failed attempts than successes, but I didn't stop dreaming. I'm so grateful for that because if I had I would have missed the opportunity to write this book in an effort to push others into their destiny. Most important, I would have missed out on the blessing of seeing some of my mentees and coaching clients successfully jump and grow their wings on the way down, and of seeing their lives completely transformed as a result of my support.

One of those mentees whom I am extremely proud of is Dr. Katrina Esau. When we first started working together, she was one of my most resistant mentees because she could not get out of her head and see her greatness. She was my truest example of what we call having *analysis paralysis*. With her permission, I conclude this chapter with the part of her story of how she took my advice to heart, and of how, when she finally jumped, she didn't stop jumping. I couldn't be more proud of how she evolved and the journey she is on today.

Dr. Katrina's Story

JUMPING OUT OF HER ANALYSIS-PARALYSIS

For nearly two years, Dr. Katrina followed me on social media, on my website, and in person. She would show up at conferences and events where I was keynoting, attend my webinars, and read all of my books and articles. She would ask questions when the opportunity allowed as our paths crossed at the church we both attended. She did all of this before we ever made our mentor-mentee relationship formal. And since we made it official I have seen a tremendous shift in her thinking, and seen her dreams soar to new heights. With her permission I am sharing a part of her journey as my mentee.

When I first met Dr. Katrina she was contemplating her next career move and seeking guidance about her role as a leader (both at work and at church). She had been a project manager for more than ten years and enjoyed job security, a steady paycheck, and a familiar routine. This was important to her because she needed everything to be perfectly clear and consistent, and she needed to feel in control. But she knew she wanted more; she was just scared to pursue it. For years she had con-templated being an entrepreneur, but she was adamant with me that she was neither ready nor prepared. In addition, the thought of going weeks or even months without income and the fear of becoming home-less or not being able to provide for her family petrified her and kept the thought of entrepreneurship in the distance.

Dr. Katrina continued to listen and watch my journey as an entrepre-neur. She would ask questions about how I handled certain challenges and what I thought of certain ideas she had. She was enamored by the authentic way I would share my personal stories publicly. She had such a compelling story herself, about surviving infidelity in her marriage, ex-periencing marital rejuvenation, and going through her personal trans-formation. I implored her to write her story and advised her to consider that her story could be a part of her business endeavor.

One of the most common pieces of advice I would give her was the same advice that Les Brown had given me a decade earlier: Jump and grow your wings on the way down. She was more than ready and had credentials very similar to mine. She was a certified project manager, a twenty-year career professional; she had been working two jobs since the age of thirteen, possessed an earned a doctorate degree, was a pro-fessor at a college, and had numerous other gifts and skills. I knew that all she needed was more courage and confidence, so I began to mentor her through a process to help her build both.

She began to understand that she didn't have to jump all at once; she could continue working her full-time job and take baby steps over time. She started by creating a list of all the "What if?" questions she had and all the things she feared about entrepreneurship. Then she created a separate list of how to overcome them. For example, her num-ber one fear was, What if I don't make enough money to provide for my family? To overcome this fear, she could save six months' worth of income to cover her expenses if a contract or opportunity didn't come. She also wrote down her vision statement so that she had clarity and could stay focused on the goal.

Her confidence was building and she was feeling more like she could achieve her dream of entrepreneurship. The last push came when she attended a conference hosted by Bishop T. D. Jakes and heard his open-ing message entitled "Jump." It couldn't have been more timely and affirming of all that she had been hearing me tell her over the years. It was the last push she needed to jump after years of my pulling teeth, persuading, and pushing her out of the nest.

A year later, still fighting her fears, Dr. Katrina put one foot in front of the other and jumped! The first step she took toward achieving her goals was to sign up for a writing course that guided her through the book writing and publishing process. She set out to publish a journal but ended up completing both a book and a journal in about six weeks. It was a lot of work trying to market the book and to juggle all of her other responsibilities as wife, mom, and full-time worker, but she was growing her wings on the way down. She jumped and started doing live interviews and keynote speaking; she jumped and launched an online academy to teach her principles to couples struggling with infidelity; and she jumped and negotiated a promotion on her job.

She still had lots of "What if?" questions, such as What if no one buys the book? What if I'm not able to get coaching clients? What if this isn't what God really wants me to do? and How will I do this and continue working my day job? But by now she had learned to shift the questions to What if it does work? and What if it helps others in their marriage? Every time things got tough and she wanted to give up, she would revisit the *why* that she had written in her vision statement.

Today Dr. Katrina admits that the payoffs of her jumping and con-tinuing to jump have been life-changing. She is still working her full-time job as a project manager, and she is learning that she can pursue her dreams and goals in steps and phases that work best for her. Jump-ing has unleashed a greater drive within her and has opened up new streams of income. She admits that jumping has also given her more confidence, caused her to invest more in her self-development, and revealed a creativity she never knew she had. More important, it has enabled her to help spouses and strengthen marriages that were dealing with the hurt and pain of infidelity.

Chapter 8

THE PAYOFFS OF
LIVING BEYOND "WHAT IF?"

A Recap of My Journey

I opened this book by sharing the vivid imaginations and dreams I had as a child, a teenager, and into young adulthood. Back then I didn't have any limitations, fears, or worries, and everything seemed possible. At a young age many of the childhood dreams I had became reality. I had not yet experienced any major disappointments that caused me to believe I couldn't achieve anything I imagined. Rather, my accomplishments caused me to dream bigger and keep imagining more—until a series of unexpected, unwelcomed, and unimaginable events exposed me to the "real world." I felt like a boxer being knocked against the ropes in the boxing ring of life, getting punched from the left, punched from the right, punched in the face, and then punched in the stomach. I was getting a complete beat down and the referee was starting the countdown to my demise and defeat. For more than twenty years my dreams were dealt major blows.

I suffered through and survived several near-death experiences, failed relationships, betrayal and broken trust by close friends and family, financial devastation, rejection, loneliness, career setbacks, and experiences of being minimized, marginalized, trivialized, overlooked, and undervalued while overperforming in many of my career roles. These experiences left me feeling stuck, unfulfilled, and searching for meaning and purpose. I was living neither my dreams nor the life I had imagined. In other words, I was living and surviving, but I wasn't thriving and enjoying life.

When I started my inward journey of self-development and reinventing myself, I experienced a shift, and the payoffs began to manifest. One payoff was that I entered into a new and different phase of my life in which I went on the offense instead of being on the defense. I took control of my life and felt empowered and emboldened to achieve better. I also got out of my own way. I had to do what my mentor Les Brown urged me to do for years: get out of my head so that I could step into my greatness. I removed the self-imposed limitations of procrastination, present bias, fear, doubt, and insecurity and began to get a larger vision for my life. I stopped entertaining disempowering "What if?" questions and replaced them with empowering responses that enabled me to build the courage and faith to believe in my big dreams, take them out of the nightstand, and begin to make them a reality.

Realizing the Payoffs

One of the most invaluable payoffs came as a result of developing the best possible relationship with myself and with my Creator. I discovered my purpose and passion, and established my life plan, which yielded greater peace, confidence, and direction. I became unapologetic about being myself and no longer felt the need to please people at the expense of losing *me*. I stopped wishing that I looked like, thought like, and acted like someone else. I celebrated my own diversity and uniqueness and was able to help others embrace the same. This was the most liberating and rewarding experience on the entire journey.

I confronted my fears and developed the courage and determination to take more risks and to ask for (and sometimes insist on or demand) what I deserved, such as being promoted and moving up the corporate ladder to become a senior executive, asking for an increase in salary, earning my doctorate degree before my fortieth birthday, providing for my daughter and ensuring that she was set up for success in life, becoming debt free and more financially savvy, buying my own home, winning a national pageant title, writing books, traveling all over the world, and running my own global consulting firm.

Some of these dreams were from my childhood and followed me into my adult life. Others developed over time, growing stronger and stronger and not going away. Today I understand that the dreams that remain in your heart and follow you over time and the dreams that never die are those that are tied to your destiny.

Another part of my process was that I unfollowed, deleted, unfriended, and blocked toxic and unhealthy people from my life. Then I surrounded myself with quality, supportive, and mutually beneficial relationships that led to a myriad of new possibilities and contracts, access to extensive resources, and a global network.

It was because these payoffs far outweighed the pain and hurts that I didn't give up. As hard as life got, with its many tests and trials and the many times I wanted to give up, I am so glad I didn't. Even when all hope seemed lost and I couldn't see my way out of dark situations, somehow a glimmer of light pushed me to keep fighting. I've come to learn that there are lessons in every test and trial. When you are prepared you pass the test and move to the next level in your life. When you are not prepared and you fail, you have to take the test over again and again until you pass. I've also come to realize that the battles we fight are not just for our personal satisfaction and grandeur. They are for us to learn, grow, and become wiser so that we can help others.

I'm so relieved that I didn't give up and that I took this path in my life; otherwise I would have missed out on another important and rewarding payoff: to impact and inspire those assigned to cross my path by sharing my story. I know that sharing the most personal parts of one's life is not easy and comes with some risks. At first I was a bit apprehensive about being so open in sharing the painful, hurtful, and embarrassing parts of my past, but I came to realize that what doesn't kill us makes us stronger and wiser. Our past doesn't have to determine our future if we learn from it.

As I grew older, matured, and healed, I understood that I had been through and survived so much for a reason. It made me a better person and it caused me to take nothing for granted—to live each day with gratefulness and intention and to live it to the fullest. Today I don't look like what I've been through. There is more good in my life than bad. There are more successes than failures. And because my perspective changed, when bad things happen today I look at them differently.

Dreams Still Get Disrupted

Even on this side of my journey, yes, I still experience setbacks and unexpected disruptions. This is called life. Just a few years ago I went through a devastating relationship experience that completely caught me off guard. I wasn't looking for a relationship at the time because I was so busy growing my business and traveling around the world. I happened to meet him on one of my trips.

I decided to let my guard down and open my heart to the possibility that a dream I was still waiting to have fulfilled—to live happily ever after with my "Mr. Right"—could be right in front of my face. The relationship started out beautifully, just like a Hallmark movie, with everything falling into place. The chemistry was there, we had similar goals in life, we were both soaring in our businesses, we talked about everything, and we complemented each other in so many ways.

But within a year this dream turned into one of my worst nightmares. Through a series of events that exposed a plethora of his secrets and lies, insecurities, mental instability, and personal inadequacies, none of which he was honest about, the relationship ended abruptly. It left me confused, hurt, and feeling like I had been hit by a twenty-ton truck and left on the side of the road like roadkill. Yes, the disempowering beliefs resurfaced, the doubts and fears returned, and the humiliation and pity party started—and it went on for months. I kept a smile on my face in public while privately I cried myself to sleep at night.

With the help of wise counsel from my closest confidants, sound legal advice, and lots of prayer, I got through it and ultimately realized that I had dodged a bullet. I finally fully recovered and healed from it, and I learned so many lessons from that experience that it deserves to be told on its own one day. So that dream of finding my Mr. Right remains unfulfilled, yet I am determined to keep hope alive.

I also still believe that my other dreams will be fulfilled, such as attaining certain financial goals, growing my business to another level, traveling to other places around the world, launching my own podcast or online show, to name a few. The point is that as long as we are alive and breathing, there is still more for us to do. We still have a purpose and relevance, and no matter what disruptions we experience we should not stop dreaming and believing.

Another major disruption that caused me to regress into fear, anxiety, and despair even while writing this book was the global pandemic of 2020–21. Who can ever forget it? Within a few days my entire life and business were turned upside down, as was the case all over the world. Contracts were put on hold, events that I was scheduled to speak at were canceled or postponed until further notice, clients' businesses were shut down, scheduled coaching sessions were canceled, and all forms of income seemed to come to a dead stop.

Yes, panic immediately set in. A few times I found myself pulling off onto the side of the road of life and wondering and praying, "God, what am I going to do now?" Eventually I recalled my past victories and drew on my lessons learned (so as not to repeat the same mistakes), and I got creative. I had to look at things through a different lens. I couldn't look at them as if I were about to lose the business I had worked so hard to build, but I had to shift my thinking and look for ways to innovate and meet client needs in an unprecedented new reality.

After months of trying to recover and figure it out, my team and I finally found a way to do just that. We turned every product and service into a virtual and hybrid offering that could be delivered in multiple formats. We developed new and relevant content that clients needed to help their workers thrive in a new environment.

Additionally, I pulled on my own network and personal board of advisers for support, and before I knew it my internal GPS had recalculated, and both myself and my business got back on track. It was a catastrophic experience that affected me personally, and millions of others around the world, and my heart still breaks for the many lives that have been disrupted and lost as a result. I am just grateful to have survived.

Amid these disruptions I have come to realize that no matter how much you think you have evolved, life has a way of continuing to test you and throw you curve balls. When that happens, you have to be ready to duck or strike back. I have come to understand that life is not what happens to you; it's what you do with what happens to you. And the lessons, the wisdom, and the successes that come from your experiences are not to be stored in a bottle, put on a shelf, or hidden under the covers. They shouldn't be the best-kept secret. They should be shared with others as testimonials that bring hope, light, and fulfillment. Today I share my stories all over the world with people from various backgrounds, cultures, beliefs, languages, and personalities. They seem to resonate across all ages, stages, and phases of life.

Yes, I believe that in life people are assigned (or destined) to cross each other's paths for a reason—that we are each meant to transfer something to the other. It's been said that people come into our lives for a reason, a season, or a lifetime. I have been blessed and inspired by so many who have shared their stories with me after hearing my story. The wonderful payoff is that they continue to affirm that my journey was not in vain, and as fate would have it they were waiting for me to get to the other side of that journey just so I could pass on the lessons, the wisdom, and the encouragement to them. So, as I come to the conclusion of this book, I want to share two more compelling and inspiring stories—those of Dr. Alexandria White and Lisa Assetta—that I hope resonate and push you closer to realizing your dreams.

Alexandria's Story

"BE BRAVE EVEN WHEN YOU'RE SCARED"

She was born on the southside of Chicago, the only girl of six children and a first-generation college graduate. While in high school, she met and fell head over hills in love with an older man and ultimately got engaged to him at her high school graduation party. She was accepted into the University of Mississippi but almost avoided attending because it would mean being away from him. But Alexandria went, and made the best of a new situation.

She was a very social person so she immediately got involved in school activities. She became an orientation leader, which taught her everything about the campus and provided extra money and free housing in the summer. She also became a football recruiter, which allowed her to be around the players and attend all of the games, which was a big deal in the South. With all of these activities going on and trying to maintain a relationship, her grades suffered. She was put on academic probation and decided to change her major from fashion merchandising to family and consumer science. This move turned out to be a benefit because it helped explain some family and personal issues that were all too familiar. However, it didn't help her break away from old high school friends who were neither academically focused nor supportive of her education efforts. Eventually her grades suffered even more as she continued to hang out with them just to "fit in."

While she was away at school her fiancé began to complain about everything, from her classes to her spending too much time in study sessions to the outfits she wore. Soon he also accused her of sleeping with the professors and became verbally abusive. Alexandria was so blinded by love, however, that she mistook his insecurity, abuse, and controlling ways as endearing and loving. In her second year of college she got pregnant by her fiancé and suffered a miscarriage. The relationship didn't improve; it got worse. His complaining and accusations went on for months, until one day it escalated into violence. One night he drove two hours to her campus apartment and physically attacked her by choking her until she lost consciousness and the apartment looking like a construction zone.

Fortunately Alexandria had told a close friend prior to this incident that he was threatening her and she was afraid he might turn violent that night. The friend kept watch over her apartment that evening by driving past periodically. She called the police when she heard screaming, and they responded immediately. As a result, Alexandria abruptly left college without contacting any of the school's personnel or her professors to explain her sudden departure.

She left the state of Mississippi, running for her life. She had to be brave even when she was scared. She left behind a large school bill and a 1.1 GPA. Yes, that's what I said—a 1.1 GPA. As she shared all of these details, she went from a serious tone to laughingly admitting that she even earned an F in jogging. This decision would later come back to haunt her in many ways. Most immediate were the effects that the physical and verbal abuse had on her mental state, the fear she felt for months that her ex-fiancé would find her, and the humiliation of loving someone who could attempt to take her life.

Then it was feelings of failure that tormented her—being a first-generation college student who didn't take her academics seriously and dropped out. Feelings of self-doubt and low self-esteem became her daily disposition. She suffered from many disempowering "What if?" questions such as, What if I continue to perpetuate generational poverty in my family and remain dependent on government assistance? What if I fail in college again? What if my ex finds me and assaults me again? What if I can't pay my college tuition? And so on. These questions plagued her for years and drove her to place limits on herself while putting many of her dreams on pause.

She relocated to Indiana after being invited by a good friend who offered her shelter and safety from her ex-fiancé. Eventually she and the friend became romantically involved and had a daughter together. Additionally, due to a tragic incident in her family, she was named legal guardian of her two younger brothers and became a "mom-sister." For three years she worked different jobs, but none seemed to work out, mainly because she lacked an education.

Eventually she landed a job at a bank. She worked there for a few years and loved it but advancement was limited because she did not have a degree. This situation was the push she needed. She had three dependents to care for, she had seen the consequences of some of her decisions, and she knew that a degree was her ticket to greater opportunities. She was ready to take her education seriously and was committed to finishing what she started. So, at age twenty-six, five years after miscarrying a child, after being nearly choked to death by her fiancé, and after making a sudden exit from college, relocating, and starting over in another state, she applied to Indiana University. But there was another problem. She had a 1.1 GPA on her transcript from her previous college and owed more than $12,000, so the University of Mississippi would not release her transcript. To make things worse, Indiana University wouldn't accept students from other universities without a transcript or fully paid bill. Alexandria was desperate. She petitioned the school to make an exception by telling her story. As fortune would have it, they agreed to make an exception and accepted her enrollment on a probationary basis, on the condition that she pay her bill at the University of Mississippi.

Alexandria knew she couldn't screw up this opportunity, and now she had three other reasons not to—her daughter and her two brothers. Her determination paid off and her life began to take a turn for the better. In her first semester, she earned a 3.6 GPA and went on to be placed on the dean's list for three consecutive semesters. She applied to be and was accepted as a McNair Scholar. She began to imagine herself beyond receiving a bachelor's degree, seeing herself as a doctor. Later she also applied for and was accepted into the Delta Sigma Theta sorority, mainly because of her grades, her personal testimony of overcoming so many adversities, and her persistence to excel.

Alexandria would continue to show this kind of persistence as life continued to throw obstacles and personal attacks at her self-confidence and courage. When the global pandemic hit in March of 2020, she joined the millions of people who were furloughed from work. Fear set in immediately and she started to rehearse those "What if?" questions again: What if I end up back in a one-bedroom apartment and have to share the bed with my children? What if I end up on government assistance again? What if I get the virus and end up with a boatload of medical bills? What would my children do?

These and other questions plagued her and nearly took her peace of mind. But drawing on the lessons from her past, she stood up to the fears and the uncertainties and began to answer her disempowering questions, recalling that she had made it through worse and survived. She began to have a conversation with herself and with her God and was determined to keep her eyes on the future and not dwell on her failures. Her fear and desperation turned into creativity and innovation.

She recalled the dreams she had that were deferred and derailed and thought, "Now is a do-or-die situation and if ever I needed to make this dream happen it is now." She decided to start her own business as an independent consultant. She reached out to previous coworkers, professors, and friends and sought referrals for clients. A new consulting and training company was birthed, and it has enabled her to take care of herself and her children without losing her home, having to share a bed with her kids, and having to rely on government assistance. She overcame her fears and her doubts and demonstrated what it means to "be brave even when you're scared." As Alexandria shared some of her life story with me, I encouraged her to consider writing a book about it with this quote as its title. I told her I was confident it would inspire many who still suffer from fear and self-doubt and need to know they can be brave while still being scared.

Alexandria is truly a success story of what courage, determination, focus, and strength can do to move a person out of self-defeating behaviors, attitudes, and actions. She turned her negative and unfortunate circumstances (some of which were beyond her control) into new doors of opportunity. Today, as Dr. Alexandria White, she exudes enthusiasm, passion, and positivity and is living beyond her "What ifs."

Lisa's Story

"THE BEST WAY OUT IS ALWAYS THROUGH"
A THREE-TIME CANCER SURVIVOR

Lisa began her thirty-year career as an administrative professional while a newly divorced single mom. She needed a job to support herself and her four-year-old daughter. She had not attained her college degree, so her job prospects were limited. She didn't care. Her desperation to provide for her family pushed her to take risks by applying for jobs she was not qualified for and doing whatever it took to succeed. She knew she was a passionate learner and detailed-oriented, so she negotiated with a small business owner to hire her as a secretary even though she had taken only one typing class in high school. Her tenacity worked and she found her career path.

In the years that followed, she pursued other administrative jobs in customer service and eventually landed in executive support. She became an expert at what she did and was hired by multiple large corporations to support high-level executives. When one of them downsized, she was suddenly out of a good job. It took a few days to get over the shock but she quickly started a job search with the help of an outplacement firm. She also utilized her strong network of colleagues in her industry and community and called on favors. After five months of searching she was approached by an employment agency offering her a position to support the office of the CEO of a major airport. After an extremely thorough vetting process that took months to complete, she was hired.

Lisa was ecstatic and in awe that she had landed such a prestigious job, considering where she had started years earlier. She would finally have the financial stability she desired and could now move beyond those goals and start to dream bigger. She wanted to find ways to contribute to the success of others, her organization, and her community in a meaningful way, and this job was her ticket to achieving that, or so she thought.

Her excitement was short-lived. The reality of what the job would be like hit her very quickly. Everything about it was difficult. She worked tirelessly to change that and make things easier, and she succeeded. She would tell everyone that she loved her job even with its challenges, even though it was the hardest job she'd ever had. She was constantly facing barriers with her direct supervisor and coworkers, yet she persevered with her usual determination to succeed. She had dreams of this being her last job and of retiring from it. She thought she could stay and change the place for the better.

And then the diagnosis came. It was cancer—again. She had been diagnosed with and treated for breast cancer five years prior to taking this dream job, and she had beat it. She had moved on into her future and never looked back. Now another cancer diagnosis was staring her in the face. Her focus shifted from the challenges she was facing at work to fighting this enemy that had returned. And other enemies had come with it—paralyzing fear that she might not beat it this time, and disempowering beliefs that made her ask, What if I lose my job and cannot take care of my daughter? and What if I lose my medical benefits?

It was scary even after beating it the first time, but at least she had a victory to draw on. The cancer treatments would include six weeks of radiation that would impact her ability to focus on work. She reluctantly took the time off that she needed for her treatment and recovery, but she had to. The treatments were hard, but she was determined to beat cancer again. And she did!

She was excited to return to doing the work she loved. Although she was passionate about her return, things seemed different in the office, or maybe things seemed different because she was different. Facing and fighting cancer was life-altering and Lisa believed it changed her for the better. She considered it a blessing in disguise. She was a survivor and she still had an opportunity to pursue her dreams.

She still wanted more out of her work life. More than anything, she wanted to be able to make that meaningful contribution she mentioned earlier. But now that contribution was going to be bigger—not only to her job and her community but also to the world. She cared about leaving a legacy and knew it would be lost if she stayed at her job. So she resigned from what she had considered her dream job and decided to search for another dream job. During her search she thought she had found it once. She accepted the position but quickly resigned from it. That job was definitely not "it," and she wasn't settling.

She continued her job search, and then the world started changing around her. Not only was there a global pandemic, COVID-19, but cancer struck again in her world. Talk about a double whammy! She was diagnosed with a new breast cancer less than two years after defeating her second cancer diagnosis. It was a familiar challenge, yet it was occurring in an entirely new environment. The world had shut down, with mandatory stay-at-home orders, schools closed and kids sent home to learn online, businesses closed, work getting done remotely and virtually, and access to health care limited due to rising cases of COVID-19.

Lisa had to face this reality head on amid all that was going on around her. She had fought this fight twice before, so she was ready to take it on again. The determination, positive mindset, and courage that carried her through her challenges before would give her strength to stay the course. She was determined not to be a victim. She embraced a "fighter's mentality" and knew it would sustain her. Yes, she wondered how many times a person could fight cancer successfully in a lifetime, but she accepted the challenge. As in her other battles with cancer, she followed the mantra "the best way out is always through." She learned that it was unproductive to spend time pondering the *why* of it. She was a woman on a mission.

This time, the cancer was aggressive. She would need surgery, radiation, chemotherapy, and immunotherapy to beat it—one full year of treatment. She took it all in stride; there was no other choice. She was going to do everything she could to get to the other side of this cancer. But this time she wasn't employed. She looked at that fact as good on the one hand because she could take the time she needed to get through treatment and recovery without the pressure of having to get back to work. On the other hand, it wasn't so good because she had no income. Her husband was self-employed but they would still miss the salary and benefits from the types of jobs Lisa had held.

For Lisa there was nothing more important than health, so she considered it a blessing to be able to focus on it solely, maximize the benefits of her treatment, and take time to recover fully to ensure that this cancer would never return. But she still wondered, What about my dream job? How could I find it now? and Will I ever achieve my dreams?

After her surgery and before her chemo treatments started she decided to restart a business she had launched ten years before. Symbolically, on Administrative Professionals Day, she registered her company with the name Office Assistance Plus. She was a business owner again and she did this in the midst of a cancer battle! She experienced such freedom and joy by starting it, because it gave her something else to fight for; she was creating her own legacy.

Lisa started a blog and became active on social media to connect with followers and build a community where together they could face life, work, and world challenges. Today, on a weekly basis she shares stories about her cancer journey to provide hope to others who are facing the same battle. She offers executive virtual assistance and virtual organizing solutions, and this is her dream job. She admits she still has a lot of work ahead to make her vision sustainable. Armed with her "fighter's mentality," the support of family, friends, and her network, she is still fighting her battle with cancer, but she is winning it and excited about her future. Lisa believes that she can do anything. She believes that her dreams are possible and is on her way to living beyond "What if?"

These and all of the other stories I have shared throughout this book illustrate significant resilience, determination, and fortitude in the midst of life's worst circumstances. All of us agree that if we had to go through it all over again to learn the lessons we did, to become the people we are today and have the peace of mind and fulfillment we now enjoy, we would take on the challenge.

African American author and poet Dr. Maya Angelou's first book of essays is titled *I Wouldn't Take Nothing for My Journey,* and this is exactly how I feel on this side of my journey. I know that Stephanie, Dr. Alexandria, Lisa, Dr. Katrina, Adrean, and Meghana would all agree. Over the years I've come to appreciate this slogan even more. One of my favorite hymns sums it up in these words I've made personal for myself: "Through many dangers, toils, and snares I've already come. It was grace that brought me safe thus far, and grace will lead me home."

When I look at the woman on the cover of this book, I am proud to be her. It's still hard to imagine how far I've come and, more important, how much I've overcome. Every day I wake up with such gratitude that I withstood the tests of time. I am not only a survivor, I am also an overcomer. My journey was scary at times; it was lonely along the way and I felt like making a few U-turns and taking some detours, but I'm glad I stayed the course so that today I can enjoy the rewards and payoffs of living beyond "What if?"

Conclusion

NOTABLE QUOTABLES TO LIVE BY

*O*ftentimes people pay me a compliment by saying they are living their life vicariously through watching me live mine to the fullest. Others say they wish they had my life. This means there are still folks out there searching for significance and meaning and not realizing their dreams. That's why I believe this book is so timely and apropos. I have been where they are and I know the feeling of wanting something better for your life but looking at your circumstances and feeling like your hands, mind, and pockets are tied, and even though you can visualize it, you still can't see it. It's a very frustrating, deflating, and hopeless feeling.

As I was writing this book I found myself reliving a lot of painful and unfortunate incidents as I laid bare my life's experiences. But writing also allowed me to reflect more on how far I really have come. Turns out that writing this book was also cathartic for me and reaffirmed the steps I took to release my limitations so I could now be living my dreams. It revealed just how much I've learned about myself, about others, and about life.

Here I've summarized those lessons in the form of what I call "Notable Quotables to Live By," which may become my next book. Additionally, at the back of the book is a discussion guide I developed for your reference. It provides a series of reflection questions based on where you are on the road of life.

I hope you will implement some or all of these "quotables" in your life, and I pray they bring you new meaning, greater clarity, and a sense of purpose and fulfillment, as they have for me.

Notable Quotables

1. Life is 10 percent what happens to you and 90 percent how you respond to what happens to you.

2. Don't just *go* through it, *grow* through it.

3. We are born with only two kinds of fears: the fear of falling and the fear of a loud sound. All other fears are learned.

4. You're either living your dreams or living your fears.

5. Failure *is* an option. Learn to fail fast and fail forward.

6. Failing at something doesn't make you a failure, nor does making mistakes make you a mistake.

7. What you resist will persist.

8. If you don't learn from your mistakes you are doomed to repeat them.

9. Life is like taking a test at school. If you pass, you move to the next level. If you fail, you have to repeat the class.

10. Opportunities never look like opportunities. They come brilliantly disguised as problems and challenges awaiting a solution.

11. Your dream must be bigger than your fear.

12. It's one thing to be alive, it's another thing to be living.

13. In life not everything is meant to be forever; some things have an expiration date, and we must discern when that time arrives.

14. You cannot conquer what you aren't willing to confront.

15. We create our own reality by the way we speak.

16. True success and happiness come from becoming the highest, truest, and most complete version of ourselves and the purpose for which we were born.

17. Even when you've had a phenomenal year of success you cannot park there and become complacent.

18. What lies behind you and what lies ahead of you are tiny compared to what lies within you.

19. Purpose is so personal that no one else has been designed to do what you were born to do.

20. The only thing keeping us from getting what we want are the messages we keep telling ourselves and those we keep believing.

21. Relationships are the new currency.

22. Imagination is the most powerful tool we have.

23. Get out of your head so you can step into your greatness.

24. Become a producer and not a procrastinator.

25. Nobody likes to follow a parked car.

26. We are the sum total of our thoughts, beliefs, and confessions.

27. Most people die at age thirty and don't get buried until age eighty-five.

28. Procrastination will never allow you to live the life you've always dreamed of. It is an epidemic that can be cured and corrected only if the underlying root causes are discovered and conquered.

29. If fear is a learned response, we can unlearn and relearn a different response.

30. It's not just what you know or who you know but what they know about you.

NOTES

Chapter Two

1. Jaffe, E. (2013, March 29). Why wait? The science behind procrastination. Accessed August 8, 2020, at https://www.psychologicalscience.org/observer/why-wait-the-science-behind -procrastination
2. Clear, J. (n.d.) Procrastination: A scientific guide on how to stop procrastinating. Accessed August 8, 2020, at https://jamesclear.com/procrastination
3. Spencer, A., & Seaver, M. (2019, August 27). Want to train your brain to stop procrastinating? Read these tips from a neuroscientist. Accessed October 1, 2020, at https://www.realsimple.com /work-life/life-strategies/time-management/procrastination
4. O'Donoghue, T., & Rabin, M. (1999). Doing it now or later. *American Economic Review*, 89(1), 103–124.
5. Bancroft, S. L., Weiss, J. S., Libby, M. E., & Ahearn, W. H. (2011). A comparison of procedural variations in teaching behavior chains: manual guidance, trainer completion, and no comple- tion of untrained steps. *Journal of Applied Behavior Analysis*, 44(3), 559–569.

Chapter Three

1. Gandhi, M., and Fischer, L. (2002). *The essential Gandhi: An anthology of his writings on his life, work, and ideas*. Vintage Books, 278.

Chapter Five

1. Bridges, W. (2004). *Transitions: Making sense of life's changes*. Hachette Books.

2. Campbell, K. (2018, January 5). How to make big health gains in the new year. *U.S. News & World Report*. Accessed December 5, 2020, at https://www.usnews.com/topics/author/dr-kevin -campbell

Chapter Seven

1. *USA TODAY Sports*. (2016, June 3). Thirty of Muhammad Ali's best quotes. Accessed November 27, 2020, at https://www.usatoday.com/story/sports/boxing/2016/06/03/muhammad-ali -best-quotes-boxing/85370850

ACKNOWLEDGMENTS

People often ask me what the key to my success is. My answer is an emphatic *family, friends, and faith*. For every important milestone in my life these three forces have been my anchor and my source of strength.

I want especially to thank my dad and mom and my three brothers for your unwavering and unconditional love and for the closeness we share as a family. You have always had my back. You have been my backbone and my cheering squad and have propelled me to overcome every obstacle and adversity I've faced and step into my greatness with boldness, courage, and perseverance.

To my daughter, Gabrielle Victoria, you are so gifted, talented, grounded, and beautiful inside and out and I am SO proud of the woman you have become. The reason I have worked so hard throughout my life is to make you proud of me. You are my love and my legacy. I love you beyond words.

And most important, I thank God for sustaining me and blessing me to live a life beyond my limitations and my "What ifs." I will continue to serve you until the day I transition from this life to my reward. I am eternally grateful for the lives I was fortunate to touch.

This book is dedicated to you all
with my sincerest love and thankfulness.

INDEX

ABOUT THE AUTHOR

Dr. Shirley Davis is an accomplished corporate executive, workforce expert, international speaker, certified leadership coach, and master of reinvention. She has consulted, coached, and presented to leaders at all levels, including boards of directors and C-Suite executives. She has also worked in more than thirty countries around the world across all industries and business sectors. She delivers high-energy, high-content, and high-impact speeches and solutions that empower individuals to achieve greatness and organizations to build more inclusive and world-class cultures where *all* talent can thrive.

Dr. Davis is also president and CEO of SDS Global Enterprises, Inc., a strategic development solutions firm that specializes in HR strategy development, talent management, organization transformation, diversity and inclusion, implicit bias, leadership coaching, and personal and professional reinvention.

Dr. Davis has more than thirty years of business, leadership, and human resources experience and has worked at several Fortune 100 and Fortune 50 companies in various senior and executive leadership roles in sales, operations, banking, retail, manufacturing, utilities, and financial services. Her last role prior to launching SDS Global was as global vice president of diversity and inclusion and workplace strategies for the

Society for Human Resource Management (SHRM), the world's largest HR association.

She holds a bachelor's degree in pre-law; a master's degree in HR management, and a Ph.D. in business and organization management with a specialization in leadership. She is certified as a senior HR professional through the Human Resources Certification Institute and the Society for Human Resource Management. Additionally, she is a Certified Speaking Professional through the National Speakers Association, a designation bestowed on fewer than 20 percent of speakers worldwide. She is also a certified leadership coach through the International Coaching Federation.

Dr. Davis has been featured and quoted on NBC's *Today* show, CNN .com, *National Public Radio,* and *Fox TV,* and in the *Wall Street Journal, Black Enterprise* magazine, *The Washington Post, HR Magazine,* and *Inclusion Magazine.* She has also been honored with numerous awards.

She is the best-selling author of *Reinvent Yourself: Strategies for Achieving Success in Every Area of Your Life* and *The Seat: How to Get Invited to the Table When You Are Over-Performing but Undervalued.* Additionally, she is a popular featured LinkedIn Learning author of four leadership courses: Inclusive Leadership, Leadership Foundations, Developing Accountability as a Leader, and Building a Diverse Professional Network.

She is a former Miss District of Columbia, Mrs. Oklahoma, and Ms. Virginia, and in 2000 won the national title Ms. American United States. Dr. Davis is active in her local community and an ordained minister and elder. She sits on several national boards and resides in Tampa Bay, Florida.

For more information or to book Dr. Shirley Davis for your next event, visit her website at www.drshirleydavis.com.

ABOUT SDS GLOBAL ENTERPRISES, INC.

SDS Global Enterprises, Inc., is a woman- and minority-owned C corporation providing strategic development solutions (SDS) that enable organizational leaders to build high-performing and inclusive cultures that thrive in a competitive and changing environment. We specialize in such areas as HR strategy development, talent management, diversity and inclusion, implicit bias in management decisions, leadership development and coaching, personal and professional reinvention, and organization/culture transformation.

With more than twenty-five years of experience and proven results, we continue to be a highly sought-after resource for many organizations. We are headquartered in Tampa Bay with offices in the Metropolitan Washington, DC area. In recent years we have expanded our offerings and our reach to various industry sectors and geographic locations, including outside the United States, including Canada, Africa, Europe, Latin America, Asia, the Middle East, and the Caribbean.

Additionally, SDS Global Enterprises, Inc. has passed the rigorous scrutiny of the Society for Human Resource Management (SHRM) and the HR Certification Institute (HRCI) and has earned its Preferred Provider Certification. This important certification means that SDS Global Enterprises' programs meet the standards and requirements of the HR profession's Body of Competency and Knowledge instituted by SHRM as well as the standards and criteria set forth by HRCI. Professional development credits (PDCs), recertification credits, and certificates of completion for programs provided by SDS Global Enterprises may therefore be awarded.

SDS's team of expert facilitators, coaches, and consultants were all personally selected (not the result of an open recruiting call). They all possess impressive and extensive credentials in human capital development. They are not only consultants and coaches but also former senior vice presidents/chief human resource officers, certified executive and leadership coaches, chief diversity and inclusion officers, officers of the court, police captains, heads of training and development and professional standards, academicians, HR strategists, and OD consultants. They bring a wealth of practitioner and hands-on experience beyond consulting. They understand organizational structures and hierarchies, strategic thinking and planning, political and regulatory complexities, culture transformation, and people management challenges.

For a full list of expert services, visit us at
www.sdsglobalenterprises.com.

LIVING BEYOND "WHAT IF?"

Release the Limits and Realize Your Dreams

By Dr. Shirley Davis

I hope that as you read this book you not only resonated with the many stories I shared but also found inspiration and guidance for your own journey. As we travel this road of life, we must recognize that we are all at different junctures and mile markers on the road toward realizing our dreams. It is important for us to take inventory of where we are and how we arrived at this place, and then begin to recalculate our lives for better or different results.

Here I use an analogy to describe four types of travelers I've met while on my own life's journey. I affectionately gave them each a name based on where they are currently. As you review these types, I invite you to select the traveler's journey you identify with most on the road of life. On the basis of your answer, use the corresponding questions for reflection, discussion, and action planning.

Note: Some of the same questions may appear under different travelers because they are relevant for those travelers' consideration.

Wandering Wanda and Peter Procrastinator

You may have been on your way to a destination but pulled over onto the side of the road because you were either lost, wandering, or trying to figure out which direction to take. You may have broken down on the road of life and need a repair. Perhaps you are even waiting for a tow to the nearest filling station. You should ask yourself these questions:

1. Think back to when you were a kid. What did you dream of or imagine doing or becoming, or where did you imagine going?

2. How did life's turns, twists and transitions impact your dreams?

3. What dreams do you keep procrastinating on? Why?

4. What does your future self wish your present self would stop doing now?

5. What are three of your most pervasive disempowering "What If?" questions? What responses can you use to address those disempowering questions?

6. What do you fear the most in life and why?

7. How have your fears kept your dreams on pause?

8. What fears have you confronted head on in the past two years? How did you confront them?

9. If we are born with only two fears, which fears did you learn? How?

10. What is your purpose statement?

11. What keeps derailing your ability to live your purpose?

12. What percentage of New Year's resolutions do you achieve each year?

13. What ritual or practice do you engage in to reflect on and assess your life?

14. What are the values you live by?

15. Which stage of William Bridges' three stages of transition model— Endings, the Neutral Zone, or New Beginnings —is easiest for you to accept? Which stage is most difficult to accept? Why?

16. How well do you manage change personally? How well do you manage change at work?

17. If you were to create your life plan, what would be your overarching goal for the next year?

18. To what extent are you in a good relationship with yourself?

19. How diverse is your professional network? How has it contributed to your success?

20. Who else should you include in your network?

21. Jumping requires us to take calculated risks. Which risks have you avoided taking? Why?

Mike Makesure and Rita Riskaverse

You may be driving in the slow lane of life, taking it easy, and taking no risks. You want to guarantee that no mistakes or wrong turns are taken, so you anticipate, contemplate, and hesitate to a fault. You should ask yourself these questions:

1. Think back to when you were a kid. What did you dream or imagine doing or becoming, or where did you imagine going?

2. How did life's turns, twists and transitions impact your dreams?

3. What dreams do you keep procrastinating on? Why?

4. What does your future self wish your present self would stop doing now?

5. What are three of your most pervasive disempowering "What if?" questions?

6. What responses can you use to address those disempowering questions?

7. What do you fear the most in life and why?

8. How have your fears kept your dreams on pause?

9. What fears have you confronted head on in the past two years? How did you confront them?

10. If we are born with only two fears, which fears did you learn? How?

11. What is your purpose statement?

12. What keeps derailing your ability to live your purpose?

13. What percentage of New Year's resolutions do you achieve each year?

14. What ritual or practice do you engage in to reflect and assess your life?

15. What are the values you live by?

16. Which stage of William Bridges' three stages of transition model—Endings, the Neutral Zone, or New Beginnings—is easiest for you to accept? Which stage is most difficult to accept? Why?

17. How well do you manage change personally? How well do you manage change at work?

18. If you created your life plan, what would be your overarching goal for the next year?

19. To what extent are you in a good relationship with yourself?

20. How diverse is your professional network? How has it contributed to your success?

21. Who else should you include in your network?

22. Jumping requires us to take calculated risks. Which risks have you avoided taking? Why?

Sammie Speedracer and Urgent Spurgeon

You may be in the fast lane of life, driving with clear direction and a sense of urgency, and having no time to waste. At this juncture you should consider these questions:

1. How have some of your life's turns, twists, and transitions helped you to achieve your dreams?

2. What were three ways you responded in an empowering way to your "What if?" questions?

3. What fears have you confronted head on in the past two years? How did you confront them?

4. What is your purpose statement?

5. What percentage of New Year's resolutions do you achieve each year?

6. What ritual or practice do you engage in to reflect on and assess your life?

7. What are the values you live by?

8. Which stage of William Bridges' three stages of transition model—Endings, the Neutral Zone, or New Beginnings—was the easiest for you to accept? Which stage was the most difficult to accept? Why?

9. How well do you manage change personally? How well do you manage change at work?

10. To what extent are you in a good relationship with yourself?

11. How diverse is your professional network? How has it contributed to your success?

12. Who else should you include in your network?

13. Jumping requires us to take calculated risks. Which risks have you avoided taking? Why?

Susie Stayput and Noah NoGo

You may be that traveler who has opted to stay put, observe, or play life totally safe and not even take the trip. Perhaps you see the journey as too difficult, not worth it, or just too scary. At this juncture it is imperative that you consider these questions:

1. Think back to when you were a kid. What did you dream or imagine doing or becoming, or where did you imagine going?

2. How did life's turns, twists, and transitions impact your dreams?

3. What dreams do you keep procrastinating on? Why?

4. What does your future self wish that your present self would stop doing now?

5. What are three of your most pervasive disempowering "What if?" questions?

6. What responses can you use to address those disempowering questions?

7. What do you fear most in life and why?

8. How have your fears kept your dreams on pause?

9. What fears have you confronted head on in the past two years? How did you confront them?

10. If we are born with only two fears, which fears did you learn? How?

11. What is your purpose statement?

12. What keeps derailing your ability to live your purpose?

13. What percentage of New Year's resolutions do you achieve each year?

14. What ritual or practice do you engage in to reflect on and assess your life?

15. What are the values you live by?

16. Which stage of William Bridges' three stages of transition model—Endings, the Neutral Zone, or New Beginnings—is easiest for you to accept? Which stage is most difficult to accept? Why?

17. How well do you manage change personally? How well do you manage change at work?

18. If you were to create your life plan, what would be your overarching goal for the next year?

19. To what extent are you in a good relationship with yourself?

20. How diverse is your professional network? How has it contributed to your success?

21. Who else should you include in your network?

22. Jumping requires us to take calculated risks. Which risks have you avoided taking? Why?